PHILIP

START
TO
LEAD

... AND OTHERS WILL MANAGE

The right of Philip Bain to be identified as the author of this
work has been asserted in accordance with Section 78
of the Copyright, Designs and Patents Act 1988

The book cover picture is copyright to Philip Bain

This book is published by
Grosvenor House Publishing Ltd
Link House
140 The Broadway, Tolworth, Surrey, KT6 7HT.
www.grosvenorhousepublishing.co.uk

A CIP record for this book
is available from the British Library

ISBN 978-1-78623-039-3

CONTENTS

INTRODUCTION

EARLY INFLUENCES...

"Dad has minutes to live" my sister said to me as she sat in the Headmaster's office. I was sixteen years old, and in the middle of my GCSE maths exam. The first part of the exam I had just finished, the second part was after lunch. My sister and I promptly went to the hospital during the lunch break. When we arrived my father was dying but had seemed to stabilise a little. As I watched my father and my great leader in his last battle... I was confronted by my first battle. A choice needed to be made. A choice of two options and both had implications. What to do? Stay with my dying father and miss the exam, or leave him and my mother and go back to school?

Like many choices that you make there will always be plenty of observers with opinions and views on what you should do in certain situations. However, in those moments I had to make that decision on my own. I made the call... I walked out of the hospital. I went back to do the exam. Was it right or wrong? At this stage, it is neither here nor there, but a difficult decision had to be made and it had to be made alone. My great adviser was dying; the man of wisdom was going and I had to make a call. And my decision was to finish my exam. Some will think that leaving my father to finish an exam was brave, some will see it as perhaps cowardly. Some will believe that the responsible thing to do would have been to stay, and others will see my going back to school as commendable. And in a way, that's the reality of leadership: your acts of leadership will have differing opinions, perhaps polar opposite opinions! The key thing for you and for me is to not worry too much about what people think, just make sure that the decisions you make are the right ones, popular or otherwise, in the circumstances you are in. Walking out of the hospital and back to that exam hall, as I look back now, was my first act of adult leadership.

The lesson from this story is that in leadership we have to make difficult and sometimes painful decisions. Those decisions can't be answered from a text book. You have to answer them. Yes of course you can listen to advice and take counsel, but at some stage a leader has to, well, lead! Those decisions may not be easy, they could have significant implications on you and others, but they have to be made. It is you making them and it is you living with the outcomes of those decisions.

A few days after my father died, I sat alone in Bewley's in Belfast having breakfast, and the realisation that my father had gone forever hit me like a train. We had spent many a morning having an Ulster Fry in Bewley's before he went to lead others while I went to school to be led (sort of). That wasn't going to happen anymore. I was on my own. The career plan collapsed, the safety net of always having my dad to employ me or bail me out was also gone. There was nothing. However, what I gradually began to realise was that there was something that my father had left me. In one of life's brutal turns my father left me something great. My father had given me a gift. It wasn't money, an insurance policy or shares in Pizza Hut (he had brought the franchise to Northern Ireland shortly after being diagnosed with leukaemia – this is covered in my previous book *Start to Grow*). It was something much more valuable. It was priceless, something that I have to this day, and no one can take away from me. It was his legacy of leadership. These lessons in leadership he taught me both consciously and subconsciously. Through his words of wisdom, his actions, and the experiences I observed and went through with him, he instilled in me leadership lessons. These leadership lessons no school or university could ever give me. They were locked in my inner being, and could only be unlocked through the joyful and painful experiences of life. He had given me a gift and it was his legacy of leadership.

Leadership is a gift. If you are a leader you have been given that gift. With any gift, you must take it with a spirit of gratitude not reluctance. And having received that gift you should then, in all humility, remember that having been given it – you must at some stage give it back. It is a gift that is only under your care and not ownership. I remember when I won the chess school cup. I got the school chess cup. I got the gift but I had to hand it back to the next winner after a year. It was not mine for ever. I got the gift, I looked after it, but always remembering that one day I would have to give it back. Your leadership will have to be handed back at some point in time – it is not yours forever. True leaders will plan to do that, will want to do that, and will ultimately do that.

LEADERSHIP IS A GIFT. IF YOU ARE A LEADER YOU HAVE BEEN GIVEN THAT GIFT. WITH ANY GIFT, YOU MUST TAKE IT WITH A SPIRIT OF GRATITUDE NOT RELUCTANCE. AND HAVING RECEIVED THAT GIFT YOU SHOULD THEN, IN ALL HUMILITY, REMEMBER THAT HAVING BEEN GIVEN IT – YOU MUST AT SOME STAGE GIVE IT BACK. IT IS A GIFT THAT IS ONLY UNDER YOUR CARE AND NOT OWNERSHIP.

As I completed my final week of GCSEs just days after my father's funeral, I had accidentally stood on a blade standing upright from a Swiss army knife (If you are over forty you probably had one). Dragging my infected leg across Belfast to my school to do my exams, a week after my father died, was pretty horrendous. However, it had to get better. And it did. It always does. The leadership journey had begun; I was now responsible for that journey, it was no longer my dad. Leadership is fundamentally about responsibility. It is about responsibility for you, others, a business, an organisation, and maybe even a country! Knowing that he was gone, I now had responsibilities. I couldn't outsource them; I had to take on those responsibilities. I had begun my leadership journey and this book is about what I learnt on the way.

Before I go any further, I want to make this clear. This book is about great leadership. And lest there be any misunderstanding - I don't believe myself to be a great leader. In fact, whether I am a leader of any sort is something for others to judge. Sure, I have engaged in leadership acts, seen it in others, experienced it and lived it out but defining me as anything in the realm of leadership will always be clouded and subjective.

Even as I write this book, as a co-owner of ShredBank with my business partner James and being involved in the governance of at least six organisations concurrently, everything that I am going to say about leadership, and particularly great leadership, is based on what I have learned on the journey. It has been through observation, experiencing it from various angles, the odd successful go at it, but mostly my understanding of the leadership journey will be through the brutal reality of failing on so many occasions to get the leadership thing sorted in my own head. So here goes...

TRUE LEADERSHIP

First of all, I personally have not met that many *true* leaders (and I have met a lot of people). In the world generally, I think *true* leaders are sadly few and far between. And of those true leaders, there are only a small fraction of truly *great* leaders. There are many of course who *think* that they are leaders but in reality... in the day to day outworking of their "leadership" they act, think, behave and operate in reality more like managers. And let me make this very clear from the outset, being managerial is not a negative thing at all. Managerial behaviour is necessary and of equal importance to leadership. Leaders need managers and managers need leaders. However, the point is that, regardless of a title, some will behave more managerially, rather than acting out the leadership role they have been given. And indeed, conversely, some people will act more "leadership orientated" despite their designated managerial role.

People can coin themselves as leaders because they have a budget and a bunch of people reporting to them, or because they have a leadership title like "CEO" in a business or "Minister" in a church. However, none of these titles necessarily mean that you are a *true* leader.

We typically have in our mind what a stereotypical leader should be like. We have a fixed view in our head as to the nature and behaviour of such a person. However, the type of person who fulfils the role of leader will come in all shapes and sizes. It is important to make this clear from the outset: a leader is not *exclusively* that charismatic hero who wins people over by their charm and panache and strength of character. Yes, there will of course be leaders like that; excellent charismatic communicators who fit the leader stereotype. However, to exclusively define a leader by those characteristics is wrong and potentially dangerous for your organisation. This is because if you are trying to identify future leaders in your organisation for development or promotion, you may exclude anyone who doesn't fit the stereotype leader profile - despite the fact that they are actually behaving like a true leader. Indeed it may also be that the high profile, charismatic individual who *is* in a position of leadership (because of those stereotypical traits) shows by their actions and behaviour their inability to actually lead!

As I say, leaders come in all shapes and sizes. There are some who are extroverts and others who are introverts, some are charismatic and others are the very opposite, some are great communicators and others couldn't string two words together. Don't stereotype leaders as they are drawn from a wide spectrum of people.

The title of "leader" whether self appointed or bestowed upon you, can only be yours if the reality of your day, your week, and your life is that you are involved in *true* leadership. So let's start with defining what *true* leadership means. There are many definitions out there and many different views on what makes a leader.

However, may I be so bold as to say, this is it! So here goes:

A leader is someone who creates an environment that enables goals to be achieved.

That's it. A leader is in the business of creating and building an environment that achieves goals. That environment could be a multinational corporation, a division, a start up, an SME, a church or just a two man finance team in a corner of an office. Whatever the environment is, the leader will structure it in a way that achieves agreed goals.

Therefore, quite simply, a leader is someone who creates environments that enable goals to be achieved. Managers will operate within the environment that they have been given, but true leaders will create the environment that will, they believe, enable goals to be achieved. That environment could be created from a standing start (like a start up business) which is challenging enough. However, leaders more often than not have to create an environment to achieve goals through changing an *existing* environment (for example, an established business or public sector organisation) – and that is off the chart challenging!

A LEADER IS SOMEONE WHO CREATES AN ENVIRONMENT THAT ENABLES GOALS TO BE ACHIEVED

That environment, that a leader creates and builds, essentially consists of four key areas that I will expand on later in the book – **Infrastructure, People, Organisation** and **Culture**:

- **Infrastructure**

  People need somewhere to sit! So the leadership needs to ensure that there is the right infrastructure in place for goals to be achieved. Infrastructure will include the fixtures and fittings, the tables and chairs, the IT systems and software, and all the tangible physical stuff that enables people to carry out their roles. The leader will ensure that the right infrastructure is in place, it is fit for purpose, and through planned investment it is maintained, changed and scaled according to the needs of the environment throughout its life cycle.

- **People**

  The environment, as with everything in life, needs people. These are all the individuals within the leader's environment who will be delivering the goals that need to be achieved. That environment could consist of one person or one million people. The leadership will ensure that the right people are brought together into that environment with all the right mix of attributes, skills and abilities to achieve the agreed goals. The leader will make sure that the people are the right fit for the environment and that they will be able to gel with the existing team and complement everyone perfectly. The leader's role is to ensure that the people are firstly competent and capable for the job that they have been appointed to and then that they are empowered and motivated to do great things.

- **Organisation**

  People need to be organised in order for the environment's goals to be achieved. The leadership needs to ensure that structures, systems and processes are introduced into the environment to ensure reporting mechanisms are in place; that there are good accountability and challenge functions to ensure people's goals are aligned with the greater organisational goals; that there is empowerment and delegation; and that everyone is working in harmony to ensure resources (both human and otherwise) are used efficiently and effectively.

- **Culture**

  When you bunch *people*, *infrastructure* and *organisation* together you get a culture. And the key for leadership is that the culture in an organisation needs to be innovative, flexible and risk orientated. This is in order to remain competitive, adaptive to change, and to retain and motivate entrepreneurial individuals that can come up with new ideas, innovate and ultimately enable the organisation to continue to be relevant to the market they serve in a rapidly changing world. This type of culture is automatically there at the start up stage and growth stage of a business. It has to be, as the organisation would not get off the starting blocks and survive otherwise. However, with the increasing scale and size of an organisation it becomes necessary for the leadership to introduce more structures, systems and processes to ensure the organisation is efficient and effective and scales for growth. However, too many structures and too much complexity typically starts to enter into an organisation after time and this can stifle innovation and risk taking and create a more bureaucratic culture. The ultimate conclusion of this bureaucratic slide will be the total irrelevance of the organisation to the market, and its inevitable closure. Leadership needs to strike the right balance of structures, systems and processes that tame complexity and ensure efficiency. Too many structures, systems and processes will stifle innovation and risk taking and cause the organisation to become stagnant, irrelevant and ultimately enter into a state of irreversible decline.

A LEADER NEEDS TO BE ABLE TO DEFINE THEMSELVES

My history teacher used to bring me to the front of the class and say to everyone – "What do you make of this guy Bain... what type of guy is he?" (Yep this really happened). He was trying to figure something out that I wasn't even too sure about myself. Start your leadership journey by very clearly defining who you are and what you are all about, because becoming a true leader can only happen when you have laser like clarity on what it *is* that defines you.

LEADERS CREATE AN ENVIRONMENT... THEN THEY MUST PRESERVE IT

Creating, and building and growing an environment that enables goals to be achieved is the leadership's responsibility. However, like any beautiful garden that you create and grow, it needs to be preserved to stay beautiful and lush and not wither and die. The leadership role is to look after the environment. Like a beautiful garden that needs to be conserved, preserved, fed and watered and tended to regularly - the environment that leadership has created needs the same. This book shows you how to do that.

START YOUR LEADERSHIP
JOURNEY BY VERY CLEARLY
DEFINING WHO YOU ARE AND
WHAT YOU ARE ALL ABOUT,
BECAUSE BECOMING A TRUE
LEADER CAN ONLY HAPPEN
WHEN YOU HAVE LASER LIKE
CLARITY ON WHAT IT *IS* THAT
DEFINES YOU.

LEADERSHIP MYTHS

There are a few leadership myths that I would like to dispel before we go any further. Again, for the purpose of ensuring that leadership is clearly defined to enable you to know if you are one, how to spot a leader of the future, and to make sure that people are not included or excluded from leadership due to wrong perceptions of who or what a leader is. Here are a few leadership myths:

- **The Success Myth**

  Leaders are not always successful. They may have created an environment which had a goal, but that goal was not then achieved. They may be unsuccessful in relation to any endeavour that they have been involved in - but they are still leaders!

- **The Unity Myth**

  Leaders don't necessarily lead a group of people with common goals. Leaders can lead divided parties who have different goals. However, a *true* leader will work that environment, maybe through persuasion, coercion, sheer determination or extraction to achieve whatever goal the leader has set. He or she may create an environment that drags people across the line! That is not poor leadership... it's just non text-book reality.

- **The Ethical Myth**

  Leaders may not always be good people. They may not necessarily be ethical. Dictators of the world do not lose leadership status because they are evil. If they are *environment creators* - they are leaders. Yes they may create an environment of fear and oppression, and an environment of terror (all of which are repugnant to me), but as evil and as reprehensible as they are, they still are creating an environment to enable goals to be achieved. And for that reason, they are leaders.

- **The Transparency Myth**

  Leaders may not always be that transparent. They may use subterfuge to achieve goals but, again, this doesn't mean they are not leaders. They are of course not ethical, but they are still leaders if they are creating an environment to achieve goals.

- **The Title Myth**

  You can have the title of manager and be the ultimate leader, or you can have the title of leader like CEO but act like a manager. Titles are not what define you as a leader: it is your action and behaviour that defines you. You could be a junior administrator and act more like a leader than any director, CEO or manager in your business.

I know a man who performed poorly academically, was hated by his teachers, found it difficult to work for anyone, signed on the dole after university, was close to being sacked twice, and at one point was close to facing financial ruin.

I also know a man who got a First Class Honours Degree, won many business awards over his career, grew a number of start-ups including co-founding two businesses, and is also involved in the governance of six large, highly respected organisations concurrently.

Both of these men are actually the same person - me. All of us are a mixture of successes and failures, strengths and weaknesses masked by a bit of bravado. Leaders are people who succeed and fail, who have a bunch of contradictions, who will sometimes lead and other times slip into management and then back again. They are a paradox like everyone else.

WHY BOTHER LEADING?

You have no choice. Like an artist who must paint, a musician who must play his instrument, a runner who must, well, run! Leaders must lead. It's what they do. They will lead their own shadow. So let's start to lead.

BECOMING A LEADER

HOW TO BECOME A LEADER

We have defined leadership, we have dispelled some myths and injected a bit of the reality of what leadership looks like. And as you read that, you may be saying *That's what I am*, or *that's what I could be*, or *that's what I want to be*. And if that is the case, then I want to look now at how you can actually become a leader. Let me be very clear - you will be a leader if you do what you are now about to read. Do the next section, believe in it, live it out, and then you will be the leader that you want to be. Oh, but remember, only a few people can actually do what I am just about to say! However, if you are up for it then read on...

IT'S IN THE BLOOD

I am both a nature and nurture person when it comes to leadership. To become a leader, there has to be something already there from the very start. That said, nurture is the lion share of the makeup of a leader. Nature - I can't do anything about - but I can give you my take on how to nurture it.

DETERMINE THAT YOU WILL BECOME A LEADER

Write it down somewhere that you want to be a leader and when it is that you actually want to become one. If you want to be a leader in two years' time then write it down. Determine in your mind that in two years you will be in a formal leadership position. Make sure, given the size and structure of your particular organisation, that your aim is realistic when determining the time it will take.

TELL WHOEVER NEEDS TO KNOW

Let your employer or manager know that you want to be in a leadership position within the timescales that you have determined. It may be unrealistic and they may suggest changing those timescales, but either way they need to know that you are on a leadership journey.

START CREATING ENVIRONMENTS TO ENABLE GOALS TO BE ACHIEVED

This is what a leader does - so do it! Start putting things in place that enable goals to be achieved without your input. For instance, put a process in place that enables certain tasks to happen in your absence (for example when you are on holiday), then look to put those processes in permanently. Speak to your line manager about certain tasks and functions that could be delegated. Do it sensitively though as you are not a leader yet!

DON'T GET AHEAD OF YOURSELF

People don't like individuals who are on the make, clearly wanting promotion to leader. At this point you are not in a formal leadership role so don't get ahead of yourself. Don't isolate yourself and create bad feeling among your peers by behaving like an arrogant, promotion-hungry individual. Learn the art of subtlety and I would refer to my previous book *Start to Grow* which covers the art of subtlety (now this is shameless self promotion on my part!).

HUMILITY

Be someone who asks for help. Don't be afraid or ashamed of asking for help. Be in the business of seeking out advice. Respect others' position, seek advice, thank them for their support and at all times be humble. In the famous film *Wall Street* in the 1980s, one of the stock market traders made the comment that we are only "One trade away from humility." Very true statement! It can all suddenly go in the wrong direction, so stay humble.

BE THE LAST ONE OUT

Be the first one in and the last one out, and don't ask for any extra money for doing so. Be someone who really has a sense of ownership of the organisation and a real desire to see things move forward. Be that individual who is seen to be doing *over and above the call of duty*. You need to hear that phrase *over and above the call of duty* a lot as you strive towards leadership. I heard that phrase in the early part of my career and you want to be hearing it also. Going the extra mile, setting yourself apart from the rest by pumping in those extra hours to make sure goals are achieved will always get noticed. Be balanced here though, as a diehard person that burns the midnight oil could be perceived as an inefficient lick who couldn't run a bath never mind a department - so be careful to be balanced in the "last one out" approach. It is more to do with your mindset and perceived mindset rather than actually coming home at midnight to a "dinner in the dog" message by the oven!

TAKE EVERY OPPORTUNITY

Whatever those opportunities are - take them. There could be additional training and development opportunities – take them. There could be an opportunity to head up a small project or initiative – take it. No matter how mundane or minor the opportunity is you need to take it, be seen to take it, and make the most of it to show everyone that you are someone who wants to take things forward for themselves, for others, and the organisation as a whole.

CARE FOR OTHERS

Great leaders care, so be someone who cares for others. Everyone has issues, and many like a listening ear and an understanding heart. So listen, care, understand and give help when possible to those who need it. You are showing the traits of a leader... selfless, caring, and helpful.

LOVE THE PEOPLE AND THE ORGANISATION

Show by your talk and walk that you want the best for people and the organisation. Stay late to finish important things off, make valued contributions in meetings, make sacrifices, help others, and support people who are trying to achieve individual team or organisational goals.

BUILD ALLIANCES

Build alliances both formal and informal. Make sure you are someone who thinks and works collaboratively, demonstrating that you are working together with others to achieve goals. Make friendships, build alliances with individuals and teams and try to work cross functionally with others in the business in order to ensure maximum buy-in for whatever you are doing in your current role. Hold your tongue and be nice even though others may do the very opposite to you.

BE KNOWN

I remember when I was young being a fairly anonymous character. In sports, I was always the last to be picked, in church life no one asked me to do anything, in school I was passed by for any honours or prizes. No one knew what I was capable of because they simply didn't know me. Sometimes humility can be taken to an extreme where it is counterproductive – you are so humble that no one knows who the heck you are! I was fortunate because a few significant individuals in my life "saw something," passed my name on to the right people and, well, the rest is history. However, it is important to be known. So be visible. Do things that make people go – "Oh, that's interesting!"

START TO LEAD… AND OTHERS WILL MANAGE

Don't act like a manager, live like a leader. Managers operate within the environment they are in, but leaders create environments to achieve goals. So whatever title you have – managerial or otherwise, always live like a leader in the way you conduct yourself and someone will eventually *formalise* you as a leader given it already has been happening *informally.*

DO GREAT THINGS

At the end of the day great leaders deliver great things. So you need to deliver great things! You need to be responsible for creating an environment (even if you are the only one in that environment) that delivers 20% sales growth, that brings in 15% efficiency through implementing a new slicker process into the organisation, that continually achieves and exceeds targets. You must do great things to be a great leader.

TRUST

Be careful who you trust. Seriously, is there anyone you know that you can be 100% certain will not divulge what you tell them? That doesn't mean that you don't tell people stuff, but just remember it will get out... someone else will get to know it! You have to assess the risk and see whether it is a risk worth taking to tell someone and to trust someone. The best person to tell is either yourself, or someone that it definitely won't loop back from. For example, tell your mum because she's not about to torpedo your business, is she?!

LEARN HOW TO BE A LEADER

Training is part of the learning mix but may I suggest only a small part of that mix. You will only get a bit of theoretical underpinning with training which is fine but don't focus too much. **Reading** around the subject of leadership is important but I would suggest one or two books on the subject of leadership. And for the rest of your reading look at biographies of leaders that will give you the richness and depth of understanding that you need. **Observation** is massively important. Look at great leaders, cherry-pick their good points and be aware of the consequences of their weaknesses. **Role models** are also very important, but again only look to one or two people and don't idolise them or be a carbon copy because people will see it – they will see it a mile off!

EXPERIENCE

There is no substitute for experience, and ultimately this will be what you need to be the finished article. We can talk about the leadership journey and the 'how-to's and 'what-to-do's but ultimately it is the experience and that rollercoaster ride of getting the corners knocked off you, with all the highs and lows, successes and failures that will get you to the status of leader.

SO WHATEVER TITLE YOU HAVE — MANAGERIAL OR OTHERWISE, ALWAYS LIVE LIKE A LEADER IN THE WAY YOU CONDUCT YOURSELF AND SOMEONE WILL EVENTUALLY FORMALISE YOU AS A LEADER GIVEN IT ALREADY HAS BEEN HAPPENING INFORMALLY.

THE LEADERSHIP JOURNEY

The leadership journey is like many of the country back roads in Northern Ireland – long and bumpy with lots of pot holes. Horrendous illustration but you get the idea. Here are my thoughts on the reality of the leadership journey that you are either wanting to embark on or are already experiencing.

YOU ARE ON A MISSION

You are in leadership for a purpose. You may not even know the specifics of that purpose but that will be revealed in the situations you resolve, challenges you overcome and the role that you play in making a difference. You may come out of that with friendships, endless wealth and great popularity with a trail of countless successes under your belt, or you could come out of that period friendless, or penniless, or even ill. But you have fulfilled that purpose.

If you are on the leadership journey expecting thanks for your efforts, you are in for a disappointing and rather short ride. Let me give you this example which says it all...

Winston Churchill was in my opinion one of the greatest leaders in history. As Prime Minister of the UK he took Britain through the war years of World War 2, he took the weight of a nation and a world on his shoulders, endured many failures and defeats, and ultimately the war was won under his watch. He ensured the civilised world would be free from tyranny. And what thanks did he get? How did people repay this great leadership? With a "Big thanks Winston, you are the man!" As a Yorkshire friend of mine would say *"Did they 'eck as like!"* In 1945, the UK won the war and in that year there was a general election in which Churchill stood for re-election. And who won that election that the war-winning, freedom-protecting Churchill stood for? Was it Churchill that won? No. The great British public repaid him by voting into power the Labour Party and its leader Clement Attlee who promised them all a bunch of welfare goodies. So there you go! Enough said.

Now it is not all thankless. I have a few people both past and present who are big on thanks. I love them for it because it is those encouragers who keep a leader going on the journey.

YOU WILL NOT ALWAYS BE POPULAR

At 23 years old I had my first performance appraisal. The CEO and one of the Directors were conducting it with me (who was a rather naive junior manager with a slightly inflated ego). The meeting started with the CEO saying: "A number of people don't like you!" To which I replied, "*What, they don't like me! Who? Who doesn't like me? What have I said... what did I do?*" The appraisal subsequently descended into me interrogating them as to who it was who said that, and what their problem was? I was genuinely annoyed.

Mike, the Director, turned around and asked, "Do you care?" To which I replied, "*Well yeah!*" And yes of course we must care if people don't like us - to a point. In leadership you will always have people who don't like you. And be assured, they really don't like you. Why? Dear knows! It will be for all sorts of reasons, rational and irrational, true and untrue, about you and about them, and so on. Now, do you need to spend *all* your time changing yourself and making great efforts for them to like you? No!! It's a lumpy carpet; by dealing with one lump another will emerge. However, there is of course always a need to self-examine and determine if there are areas in your life that need to be improved. You are not beyond looking inwardly at those aspects of your leadership style that may need to be tempered, altered or radically changed. However, it is also important that everyone needs to understand the brutal facts about who you are and why you do what you do! They may not like you, they may not agree with you but at the very least they need to understand what you are about – why you do what you do.

Being liked, loved, hated or whatever is not something to spend a great time of emotional energy over. Look, people will have all sorts of reasons for liking you or not liking you. There could be jealousies, anger, resentment, or they just don't like your face. Either way, do you care? If you are a leader you can't care too much!

YET THE JOURNEY CAN BE ONE OF GREATNESS

You can change the world. Yes you. Leadership allows you to do that. Yes it can at times be thankless and at times lead to you being unpopular, but that doesn't really matter because as a leader you have a great focus and a great prize. That focus is on making the world that little bit better. The gift of leadership that you have can make a difference to people, communities and even the world!

THE GIFT OF LEADERSHIP THAT YOU HAVE CAN MAKE A DIFFERENCE TO PEOPLE, COMMUNITIES AND EVEN THE WORLD!

START TO LEAD / PHILIP BAIN

THE LEADER'S PERSONAL CHALLENGES

THE CHALLENGE OF FEAR

Leaders have a lot to be fearful about on their journey. If you lead a business your fear may be competitors, cash flow drying up, industrial tribunals, or the economy collapsing. If you lead a family there are plenty of fears - fear for your family's security, health, their well-being, and so on. If you lead a government then leadership will fear making a political faux pas, there will be fear of dissension, fear of recession and fear of negative media exposure. Fears are everywhere. We live in a world that is highly uncertain. It is a world of confusion, rapid change, deteriorating economic conditions, and more uncertainties every day.

Fear is deep, deep down there with ALL leaders. What is tomorrow going to bring? We don't have the faintest idea! No clue. Leaders can't be fearless, of course they have fears. It is how they deal with the fear which is important. And here is how to do it:

- **Talk it out...**

  Fears need to be talked through with someone who can advise you, calm you, and help you to work through it. Find someone you can talk to.

- **Burn it out...**

  Burn it out of you by exercise. Run, walk, and do whatever sport you do to sweat the fears out of you!

- **Work it out....**

  Head in the sand mentality rarely works. Most of the time we have to confront our fears head on, and deal with them. By working on those issues that we fear we can perhaps minimise the fear or eliminate it altogether.

- **Reason it out...**

  95% of what you worry about actually never happens and if it does happen it most likely will not be as bad or as consequential as you feared it would be. Look back in your life – largely this will be your experience. Some fears we have are irrational and others rational. Work on the rational fears and see if you can ease those fears by talking it out, burning it out and working it out.

- **Take it out...**

  What you can't do anything about just let go. What you can do something about, put a plan in place to deal with those things that cause fear.

FEARS NEED TO BE
TALKED THROUGH WITH
SOMEONE WHO CAN
ADVISE YOU, CALM
YOU, AND HELP YOU
TO WORK THROUGH IT.
FIND SOMEONE YOU
CAN TALK TO.

CHALLENGE OF NEGATIVITY... TOWARDS YOU AND OTHERS!

It is likely that some people will have said something negative about you. Why? Well first, no one is perfect and as we are not perfect, we have imperfections and those imperfections will have been reflected on, discussed, mocked, and commented on by people. It is inevitable. It's wrong to back-stab and talk about people behind their back. However, everyone has done it and you have done it too. No one is innocent on this and you know it. The smart ones - you will never know that they are doing it; the dopey ones - you will know pretty quickly. Either way, everyone is doing it.

When you hear negative comments about someone, ask yourself this question when deciding on whether to address it with the individual that the negative comments are being directed at - is it edifying, is it constructive and can the person do anything about it? If the answers are "no", then say nothing. Someone might think that you are an idiot, incompetent and not good at leading. Do you need to hear that from them or someone else? Maybe, but more often than not I suspect you don't! Passing on negative comments may be necessary to bring that person to a realisation of shortcomings that need to be addressed. However, if the truth be known, rarely do we need to hear that someone thinks negatively about us. I think Proverbs 11 verse 12-13 sets out good principles on this matter:

> *Whoever derides their neighbour has no sense,*
> *but the one who has understanding holds their tongue.*

> *A gossip betrays a confidence,*
> *but a trustworthy person keeps a secret (NIV)*

However, it is important that as leaders we are not in some fantasy bubble of unreality with a misguided sense that all is well in the world and everyone loves your leadership. Leaders need shots of reality, we need to hear of the elephants in the room even though it may be painful to hear. Still, everyone also needs to be careful not to discourage for discouragement sake. In other words, we need to make sure we ease off on ourselves and those who lead us – it's a tough gig!

Sometimes though when you are feeling a bit broken from the waves of criticism that will inevitably come, maybe it is worth reflecting on these words I picked up from a random film I watched the other night spoken by a man who was misunderstood by his colleagues.

"Doesn't really matter much does it... the judgement of other men? I know what I have done..."

When you feel misunderstood, under attack, rejected, and friendless then maybe the words above are what you need to say.

THE CHALLENGE OF EMOTIONAL STRENGTH

Leaders need a great deal of emotional strength. The weight of responsibility, the complexity of problems, dealing with difficult people and the whole rollercoaster ride can be challenging enough on the leadership journey. Therefore, leaders need to be strong physically, mentally and emotionally. Emotional strength, I don't think, can be taught or learned. I think you either have it or you don't. And you have it because it is part nature and part nurture. The emotional muscles that you had from birth have been nurtured, strengthened and developed through the course of time. And it is that very emotional strength that you have that you will need in order to face the challenges of leadership.

However, remember that no matter how emotionally strong you are, you are not invincible. You need to protect your emotions. Make sure you know your limits, take holidays, and don't carry too many burdens or carry too much weight and pressure. Take care of yourself, and make sure as a leader you take care of others' emotional well-being. You can break someone by putting too much pressure on them. So make sure you know everyone's limits and encourage a healthy balanced lifestyle where the weight of responsibility is not stuck with one person but shared among others in the environment that you have created. As the US TV host used to say at the end of each show: "Take care of yourself... and each other."

SOMETIMES EVEN A LEADER NEEDS TO JUST CRY LIKE A BABY

Yeah, sometimes you just have to cry. Here's a personal story to explain.

I'm sorry but selling photocopiers was the worst business experience in my life. My stomach hurts even writing about this. Ok this is how the story goes. I had graduated with a first class honours degree in June, I was firing CVs around every big consultancy firm, top 100, and Northern Ireland big corporate I could find, thinking that everyone would be chomping at the bit to hire me. Ah, no! I did work my way into an interview in one of London's largest consultancy practices. The only notable event on that day was having the waitress spill half my dinner on my lap in Hard Rock cafe! I landed back in Belfast, signed on, then signed up with an agency and within two weeks got a job selling photocopiers.

Picture this. I had a briefcase in one hand, a presentation folder in the other, and a chunky mobile phone in my pocket walking the streets of Omagh. Walking from one business to the next, trying to convince them to buy a £5k - £10k photocopier range. Eight weeks in and I landed the jackpot with a proposal to sell a £12k colour photocopier. Yes!!! A very quiet, gentle, unassuming guy was keen to buy and, hey, I was keen to sell. The old adage, "It's the quiet ones you have to watch", comes to mind. This guy was a lion! Twelve round trips to Omagh, and he played me and another competitor against each other like a ring master in a circus. This guy was a genius, he had slashed the price to £5,250!! On trip twelve to Omagh, I was briefed by my Sales Manager to sign him up. When I arrived he quietly brought me into his office. He told me very quietly and very gently he had given the deal an hour earlier to the competitor. I cried.

Sometimes you just need to cry. Now don't get me wrong. I am not a crier. Maybe three times I've cried in my business life. One was the photocopier experience, another was when a former boss told me to expletive off (several times) in a moment of rage, and the third time, well I'm not sure what happened but there has got to be at least a third time as it would make me sound unemotional and cold to only have cried two times! Anyway, sometimes you just need to let the emotion out. But never ever let anyone see this.

THE CHALLENGE OF NETWORKING

Confession, I am an introvert. I am awkward in large groups. I dislike, in fact I despise parties; I am in essence a loner and always have been. Now for some who know me they will already know that about me and will be unsurprised; others perhaps will see that as a complete paradox given I am a public speaker in the business realm and lay preacher in the spiritual realm. Paradox it may be but that's who I am – odd! So what does an oddball like me have to tell anyone about networking! Well firstly, my immediate take on it is to ditch the term "networking". Networking, for me, is a term that sends out all the wrong signals. Networking implies a kind of targeted sales-orientated approach to every business event and interaction that you ever engage in. Networking implies that you prepare the night before your "target list" of event attendees, to approach them and to try and cultivate some form of relationship in order to get sales out of them at some time in the future. Networking implies wrong motives, it implies artificial relationship building, it implies people will eventually get wise to it and you will become marginalised at best and isolated at worst, because you will be known as a person who is always "on the sell"! And you really don't want to be known as that.

So let's change networking to something more human, let's just change networking to "building relationships". Relationship building is what great leaders do. They don't build relationships for sales, for opportunities, for personal development or whatever else some daft seminar or text book would say on networking. Leaders build relationships for one reason and one reason only - because it is the right thing to do. They want to build relationships because in and of itself, regardless of what comes out of that relationship, it is a good thing to form friendships and relationships with your fellow human beings.

So let's change the title of this section from "The challenge of networking" to "The challenge of building relationships." So here is how we do that:

HAVE A VISION

The journey of relationship building has already started. You have friends, and you have acquaintances, and you know people. So that already is happening. From the point of view of you as a leader or a future leader, the journey of developing new relationships may be more in its infancy. The beginning of that journey starts with being comfortable with you. I touch on this in my previous book *Start to Grow*. You don't need to undergo radical change. You are you, love you and that's it. However, you must have a vision. You must have a sense of who you are and what you are about. What are your strengths? What are your weaknesses? What is your passion? What drives you? Get a sense of who you are before you start introducing "you" to someone else.

Be careful who you build relationships with. Essentially, there are two groups we need to talk about – Giants and Sharks. The bunch in the middle is pretty much *"bleh"* and hardly matters as they are neither dangerous or amazing they are just, well, *"bleh."*

CHARACTERISTICS OF GIANTS

SELFLESS

Giants are typically people who are selfless. They have a deep sense of the importance of doing good towards their fellow man. They engage in selfless acts towards others that benefit that person but do not necessarily benefit themselves. They haven't been taught to be like this – that's just the way they are. They are concerned more with the needs and wishes of others than with their own.

SACRIFICIAL

Giants are sacrificial. They may sacrifice time to encourage, help or advise you. They sacrifice money to support you, bonus you or pay you. A giant can make big sacrifices for others even though it may impact negatively on that giant. They make these sacrifices for your good, the greater good, and to ensure things move forward. They do so because they are selfless, because they put others ahead of themselves, and because their thoughts and heart are to help others.

YOU MUST HAVE A SENSE OF WHO YOU ARE AND WHAT YOU ARE ABOUT. WHAT ARE YOUR STRENGTHS? WHAT ARE YOUR WEAKNESSES? WHAT IS YOUR PASSION? WHAT DRIVES YOU? GET A SENSE OF WHO YOU ARE BEFORE YOU START INTRODUCING "YOU" TO SOMEONE ELSE.

HONOURABLE

Giants are honest, moral, ethical, principled, right-minded, and full of integrity. These are the sorts of people you want to build relationships with. Do you want to build relationships with the opposite of this? Do you want dishonest, unethical and immoral people in your life? If you have them already, get rid of them or you will become like them. There are plenty of honourable people out there and plenty of dishonourable ones – choose carefully.

TRUSTWORTHY

A trustworthy person is someone who is reliable, dependable, honest, full of integrity, worthy of trust, honourable, principled, ethical, and incorruptible. They are a rare breed but when you find them – hold on to them tight.

CHARACTERISTICS OF SHARKS

SELFISH

Sharks are typically people who are selfish. They are totally consumed with themselves and their own agenda. Every interaction, every dialogue, and every action is ultimately about one person – them! They just simply don't care. Their actions are self-serving, they don't care about others' feelings, they won't carry other people's burdens, and they won't engage in selfless acts. It is all about them – and that is it. Hey, they may not even recognise the fact that they are selfish but then that just compounds the problem because not only are they selfish, but they lack self-awareness too.

DANGEROUS

Hard to accept, but there are people out there who genuinely are about doing people harm. I don't mean physical harm (though that might be the case), but harm in the broadest sense of the world. Sharks will want to damage your career, maybe your reputation, and maybe your relationships. Sharks are heartless, selfish and self-orientated so they won't care. They will gossip about you, spread rumours about you, befriend you for all the wrong reasons. No, these guys are all wrong for you and do whatever you can to avoid them.

DESTRUCTIVE

Sharks are not about harmony, they are about disharmony. They are not about unity as they actually go out of their way to bring disunity. They can destroy lives, businesses, relationships, organisations, friendships and the list goes on. It is because they are selfish and dangerous that they will inevitably bring destruction. Want to know if you are a shark or a giant? Look at the trail behind you: does it contain unity, harmony, peace and friendships or does it have the opposite?

PRE-EVENT PREPARATION

"Networkers" will tell you to do pre-event preparation – they will suggest getting your target list, doing background research on each one and all that nonsense. Here's my take regarding pre-event preparation – don't do any! You can do all the preparation you like but I guarantee it will come to nothing. You will get out of that event stuff you never even planned for, and you will not get stuff that you hoped for. Just go in there, build good relationships and the right things will happen.

Also, before the event, ask yourself why you are going. Are you going because you are trying to avoid actually selling?! Are you going because you need to be doing more "networking"?! Is the event relevant for you to be going to? Does it help achieve those goals that you have set? Or is it an excuse to get away for the day?!

Your time is precious, you have only a finite amount of it and therefore don't waste it going to events that are not relevant to you or your organisation.

THE EVENT

Some thoughts about when you turn up at the event:

FIRST IMPRESSIONS

- **Smile with your eyes.** My wife always tells me to smile with my eyes. Anything else is soulless and looks fake. You want to see me not smiling with my eyes – scary!

- **Eye contact.** Make sure you are not looking at their chin, or lower half, or upper half or anything other than their eyes! Don't eye pierce too much though as you might freak them out. Hey, just be natural and personable.

- **Moderate handshake.** Wet fish handshakes are out! Good firm handshake is good but not too hard and make sure your palms are dry. Anything else is not a good start to a relationship!

- **Moderate distance.** Don't be in their face and don't be talking to them from across the room. I exaggerate to make the point but just, like everything in life, keep it moderate including the distance between them and you.

- **Drop the act.** Be you. Don't be anyone other than you. Don't be all businesslike and corporate if that is not who you are. Be authentic, with integrity... and be you. It is the best option.

THE LIKEABILITY FACTOR

"Some cause happiness wherever they go; others, whenever they go!"

Oscar Wilde

- **Show an interest in their business.** People want you to know and understand them and to show an interest. Spend time getting to know them, and at least look like you care!

- **Show an interest in them.** Building relationships is about getting to know the person. Ask about the things that will be important to that person – their work, their family, and their interests.

- **Be friendly, chat, and build rapport.** Yes, do all these things and you will be likeable. Very simple but unfortunately many people fail to master this.

- **Respect their position.** Whatever position they have in business or in life, respect it. They could be high up the corporate ladder or just on the first few rungs. Respect them and respect everyone.

DON'TS...

- **Don't network** in the classic sense of the word
- **Don't sell** in any sense of the word
- **Don't pitch** to people because you certainly don't want to be pitched to
- **Don't work the room,** as people (including you) hate anyone who does that
- **Don't hand out business cards** (waste of time and also annoying)
- **Don't annoy** generally

DO'S

- **Do be relaxed** as uptight people are scary
- **Do take a leap** and break out of your comfort zone
- **Do talk to anyone** regardless of who they are (with exception of sharks)
- **Do develop existing relationships**
- **Do build new relationships** and don't just hang about with the same people
- **Do what others may not do** (take out for lunch, selfless acts etc)

SOMETIMES JUST STAY AT HOME!

Just don't go to the event. Stay at home; spend time with your partner or family or friends. Just chill. It may be infinitely more beneficial for you to do that than to run around at some daft event late into the night!

> *"You can easily judge the character of a man by how he treats those who can do nothing for him."*
>
> *Malcolm S. Forbes.*

Powerful statement and very challenging! Speaks to us all. We need to be in the business of encouraging others. I guarantee you that at least one person has discouraged you in the last month. Guaranteed! There are many discouragers out there and few encouragers. Build relationships on the bedrock of encouragement. Encourage your friends, family, colleagues, and of course those who can do nothing for you.

BUILD RELATIONSHIPS

- Family first... this is the starting point. You must get this right before anything else.
- Build on existing relationships and get new ones
- Give and don't take
- Take out to lunch
- Love to learn
- Say "Thank you"
- Keep in touch...

STAFF RELATIONSHIPS

- **Care about them...** be selfless and sacrificial when you can be
- **Lead them...** and don't manage them
- **Understand them...** by getting to know them
- **Ditch management speak** and talk normal

CUSTOMER RELATIONSHIPS

> *"They are like one of your children...*
> *a precious baby that must be cared for,*
> *loved and adored...there is no one like them*
> *and in all things they must always come first."*

Philip Bain (my quote)

SUPPLIER RELATIONSHIPS

Build strong durable relationships with high quality suppliers, and yes, push them on getting the best price, but the main goal is good, solid, enduring relationships because suppliers along with cash are your lifeblood.

BUSINESS RELATIONSHIPS

Business relationships should be centred on the following...

- Honesty
- Truth
- Integrity
- Kindness
- Patience
- Humility
- Self-control

GREAT
LEADERSHIP

THREE TRAITS OF GREAT LEADERSHIP

We have looked at the leadership journey and what it looks like but ultimately that leadership journey should not lead to mediocrity in your leadership, it should lead to greatness. And essentially that is what the rest of this book focuses on – great leadership. We have defined it, and hopefully dispelled some myths but now let us get to the meat of the matter and that is great leadership. In my experience, there are three common qualities that I have noticed in all leaders that, in my view, make them "great".

GREAT LEADERS WANT TO CHANGE THE WORLD

Great leaders have a desire to change the world and make it better. The world is in a pretty chaotic state and we need great leaders in every realm of society, not least in business, to drive change that can ultimately benefit all of us. A great leader is someone who desires to do something greater than just improve the bottom line. They want to make the world better; better for the people who work for them, for the community around them and even society as a whole. You will never be a great leader if you don't have that sense of a greater purpose to make the world better. If you walk into your office and want to manage everyone and tell everyone what to do and are itching just to manage people – then you will not inspire anyone, you will not motivate anyone and in fact, people will be demotivated.

You have the power to create an environment where people love coming to work, an environment in which people feel valued, where their opinion matters, where staff can be empowered to make decisions and to achieve things that they never thought possible. Or, you can create an environment that is filled with tension, office politics and disengagement. You have the power to create a poor working environment or a great one – that is your choice. Great leaders are about creating an organisation that means something; that people can be proud of and that makes a difference in society.

YOU HAVE THE POWER TO CREATE AN ENVIRONMENT WHERE PEOPLE LOVE COMING TO WORK, AN ENVIRONMENT IN WHICH PEOPLE FEEL VALUED, WHERE THEIR OPINION MATTERS, WHERE STAFF CAN BE EMPOWERED TO MAKE DECISIONS AND TO ACHIEVE THINGS THAT THEY NEVER THOUGHT POSSIBLE.

A great leader isn't doing it to get self affirmation, a vehicle to feel good about themselves and to give them a sense of self worth and an ego boost. Leadership is not for them to satisfy their life's desire to "lead something... lead anything". It is not to be patted on the back and be told they are great. Nor does the leadership role give them the opportunity to strut about and be *all leader like*! Great leaders don't lead for this selfish and self serving agenda. They do it because they want to make people's lives better.

GREAT LEADERS WANT TO BE REDUNDANT

Poor leaders want to be indispensable. They want to be considered critical to the company's success and love the fact that everyone waits in anticipation for their return from their two week holiday, so they can restore order to the business that has been literally shuddering in their absence. Unfortunately, this is poor leadership because they haven't created a team that can function in their absence, nor have they created systems and processes capable of running smoothly without their input. And if truth be told, many leaders want it that way. This means that these leaders haven't empowered people to make decisions, haven't delegated responsibilities, and haven't invested in people development.

What bad managers fail to realise is that they are harming their business by failing to develop their staff. Great leaders however, want to be made redundant! Great leaders see power as something that when you get it, you should do everything you can to get rid of it. Great leaders want to build capacity in the organisation and encourage others to up their game, to take on new responsibilities, to be creative, and to make decisions. They want to create an environment in which the leader is effectively not needed. If they achieve this, it allows them to think strategically and to focus on taking things to the next level. Do you as a leader want to be made redundant?

GREAT LEADERS ARE COMFORTABLE WITH THEIR WEAKNESSES

Great leaders almost always love to talk about things that they are *not* good at. Yes, self-belief is important, but I would argue having bags of humility is even more important. Poor leaders tend to hide their weaknesses. They want to give the impression that they know everything, that they need to be involved in everything and that their opinion is all that matters. Having humility means you accept you don't have all the answers and you embrace those who do! Great leaders ask for help, seek the advice of wiser heads, and they don't try to cover up mistakes. They are open and honest and regularly seek help. If you are comfortable with your weaknesses, you will be comfortable delegating, empowering, promoting and trusting people's judgement. Get comfortable with your weaknesses, and you will build a truly great team that will do things more effectively than you ever could alone.

HAVING HUMILITY MEANS
YOU ACCEPT YOU DON'T
HAVE ALL THE ANSWERS
AND YOU EMBRACE THOSE
WHO DO!

HOW GREAT LEADERS BEHAVE

STRATEGIC THINKERS... TACTICAL BELIEVERS

Leaders think strategically but also believe fundamentally in the importance of tactical decisions. They are "big picture" people through and through. The immediate issue or action is of course of interest, but of greater importance are the consequences of that immediate issue or action on short, medium and long term goals. They are visionary in the sense that their vision is broad and long. Their thinking is: "What is the impact of that decision on the long term goals of the organisation?" As they stand at the foot of the mountain, they see the tactical challenges of the rocks, boulders and brutal weather but they are more focused on looking at the top of the mountain, the opportunities of climbing the mountain, and the potential opportunities that lie beyond it.

THEY ARE ABOVE REPROACH

Many years ago, before co-founding ShredBank with my business partner James, someone once attempted to bribe me to work a move with a board in their favour. It was quite a substantial sum. The offer shocked me, I was mildly amused but I unequivocally refused. For the record, I didn't take the bribe, I wasn't tempted and nor would I ever have taken the bribe. I have done plenty of wrong things in my life, but not on that occasion. I smiled and politely declined. Leaders need to be above reproach. Money or anything offered to behave in an unethical way should be rejected outright... always. Leadership integrity has perhaps been replaced by "authentic leadership" in leadership thinking today, but although I believe authenticity is important, you could be authentically morally bankrupt! So let's put integrity in leadership back as an essential for great leadership.

THEY KEEP THEIR COOL

In short, be patient with people, they are a work in progress.

Before ShredBank, a number of years ago, one of my staff came into my office quite upset that the Chair's PA had been rude and aggressive towards her. As a young and rather impetuous business manager I got straight on the phone with the PA and told her to not ever speak to my staff in that way again. My phone rang within a minute, with the Chair of the organisation asking me politely to come up to his office. As I walked into the office, the air turned blue and I was hit with every expletive under the sun. After a couple of minutes the barrage of abuse stopped and he started to ask how I was getting on in the job!

On another occasion before ShredBank, I had to meet a purchasing manager who wanted to withdraw from a contract. I told him about the penalty fees that would be incurred as a result. On this occasion, he didn't shout or scream, he just stayed silent and stared. It was really freaky. He just stared! I sat there staring back determined not to flinch or be the one to speak first and we literally just stared at each other for what seemed like forever. One of my staff members who was with me didn't know whether to laugh or cry!

People are quick to lose it and go off the handle. Everyone is emotional, and to be a bit Orwellian about it, some are more emotional than others. Complex situations, times of crisis and conflicts can make some people react in irrational ways. They lose their cool. It is the only way they can respond. However, the knee-jerk reaction and the emotive behaviour more often than not typically inflames the situation and generally creates more heat than light! I know, I have done it many times to my regret.

However, a great leader is someone who reacts very differently. A great leader is calm. While everyone around the leader is jumping up and down, screaming and over-reacting (for undoubtedly legitimate reasons), the leader is the calm and tranquil head. Why? It's simple. That's the quality of great leadership. If the leader is bouncing around losing their cool then the ship sinks, and great leaders aren't in the business of allowing ships to sink.

The reason why great leaders keep calm is simple - a great leader is not subject to his or her emotions or governed by them. They are people characterised by self control. They are the calming influence on a dynamite situation. With this inner calm and control of one's emotions realities don't get clouded and the leader can then be focused on what the true issue in the room is.

And that is a true mark of a great leader – someone who quickly gets and focuses on the *issue in the room*. They will more clearly see the issue, how to resolve it, and then what needs to be put in place to prevent a repeat. Leaders are not out for blame, although heads may roll, but they are rather focused on ensuring the environment achieves its goal - nothing more and nothing less.

Also be patient with yourself. You are also a work in progress! Maybe your shortcomings are a source of inner discouragement or self doubt. Maybe the fact that your communication skills are not what you think they should be, or your inability to handle a situation in the way you think it should have been handled is a source of frustration. Be patient with yourself as leadership is a journey of successes and failures, sometimes doing the right thing and sometimes the wrong thing. Leadership is a learning journey. Some people are paying you to learn and they are or have been relatively patient with you, so you should at least be equally patient with yourself. I think we have exhausted the point. You get what I'm saying.

LEADERS LOVE THOSE THEY LEAD

You may be asking, "Where are you going with this, Phil?" Well let me clarify. There are, as we know, many different types of love. Love for your parents is different than love for your husband or wife. Love for a friend undoubtedly trumps love for a holiday destination. You get the picture.

The type of love I am talking about here is *sacrifice*. Love means sacrifice. Any leader worth their salt will ultimately be prepared to make sacrifices for those they lead. You will sacrifice time for them, perhaps money, and sacrifice potentially many other things for their ultimate good.

SOMETIMES LEADERS NEED TO BE CALCULATING AND UNEMOTIONAL

I remember many years ago being approached by a sizeable organisation to collaborate on a large tender for a contract. We started on the journey together but as we progressed my slice of the deal got smaller and smaller and smaller. I saw where it was headed and we were going to get squeezed almost completely out of the deal. I could have got annoyed, stamped the feet, called meetings, etc. However, I took the view... stuff it! I decided to negotiate another contract - a bigger and better one - and go into an alliance with a different organisation that was a competitor of mine. We got the contract. Don't get emotional no matter what people do to you. Sometimes you need to be calculated, unemotional, and get the contract!

LEADERS CARRY SOME HEAVY LOADS

There are some things in life you have to carry. Hard reality, but it is a fact of leadership. The bag you carry may be loss, rejection, betrayal, or pain. Of course, what strengthens you to carry that bag will be the joys, encouragements, successes and advice you get on the leadership journey. The next time something or someone hurts you, try to shake it off and work it out of your system. However, if you can't do that be prepared to accept it may be one of those things you have to carry. One way or the other - forgive them. As the wise mentor said to his protégé in the 1980s Karate Kid 2 Film *"Person with no forgiveness in heart, living is worse punishment than death."*

LEADERS ARE MASTERS

- **Be a master communicator:** Leaders need to be able to communicate their goals to their people so that everyone understands and has ownership of those goals. Leaders need to be able to engage in all ranges of communication from informal discussions by the water-cooler to communicating to a number of people at a staff meeting.

- **Be a master peace maker:** A leader is a peace maker and not an agitator. The leader will be about bringing calm and peace to conflict and stressful situations that will inevitably occur. The leader should not be like petrol on fire by inflaming situations even more. Rather they should be going into every situation (without exception) with the objective of bringing peace. The reason is firstly because it is the right thing to do, but also the absence of peace leads to heightened emotions, irrational responses and general disunity. And that is no good. A leader must bring peace.

- **Be a master problem solver:** A leader will always come to problems with a laser-like focus on trying to achieve a solution. Great leaders don't look to find blame and hang the guilty. They are fundamentally about bringing solutions to an environment of problems and difficulties.

- **Be a master delegator:** Leaders master the art of delegating tasks and duties to others and empowering them to do great things. Delegating and empowering others is part of the fundamental trait of a great leader – the desire to make themselves redundant, and to create an environment where the leader is essentially not needed. This can only happen by letting go and building up a team that complements the weaknesses of others and builds strengths through delegating and empowering.

LEADERS HAVE WISDOM, KNOWLEDGE AND DISCERNMENT (WKD)

Leaders need wisdom, knowledge and discernment (WKD). By the way I love the "WKD" acronym (not my idea, but it was a friend and great business guy called Mogue who came up with it as we were deliberating about the importance of wisdom, knowledge and discernment in leadership over a steak one evening). Without WKD you can lead nothing. Leaders deal with everything with a spirit of wisdom. Wisdom comes from knowledge and experience grounded in a desire to always do the right things. Wise heads can be on young shoulders, and foolish heads have been on many old shoulders - so age has nothing to do with it. Only wise people can be great leaders. A man or woman who is known to be wise is a great and powerful influence in any environment. This is because they bring wisdom to complex challenges, they bring wisdom to conflict and they bring wisdom to taking the organisation forward. Wisdom leads to wise decisions and lack of wisdom leads to foolish decisions. Winston Churchill once said: "Character is the habit of making right decisions."

Discernment is also important and typically only comes with knowledge and experience. Discernment is the ability to tell truth from error. And in a world that has a great deal of error and untruth in it, it is necessary to have the ability to discern in every situation and perceive where the truth lies.

LEADERS BRING ORDER

- Where there is confusion, a leader brings clarity
- Where there is disunity, a leader brings unity
- Where there is falsehood, a leader brings truth
- Where there is hurt, a leader brings healing
- Where there is disharmony, a leader brings peace
- Where there is chaos, a leader brings order

LEADERS BEHAVE IN A WAY THAT INSPIRES

How do you inspire people? People get inspired for all sorts of reasons. However, to get straight to what I believe inspires people I'd like to refer back to what I wrote in my previous book *Start to Grow*. There I maintain that leadership is about "doing the right things." In other words in all circumstances of life choose the better way. We won't always do this! I choose the lesser way countless times. However, we should always strive to choose the better way and do the right things. So we should choose peace rather than disharmony, we should choose sacrifice rather than selfishness, we should choose patience rather than temper, and we should choose wisdom rather than foolishness. We should choose responses of love, peace, kindness, goodness, gentleness, and self-control. And if we do this we will inspire others more than a multi-million-pound stock listing, global adventure or political achievement could ever do!

WE SHOULD CHOOSE
RESPONSES OF LOVE,
PEACE, KINDNESS,
GOODNESS, GENTLENESS,
AND SELF-CONTROL.
AND IF WE DO THIS WE
WILL INSPIRE OTHERS
MORE THAN A MULTI-
MILLION-POUND STOCK
LISTING, GLOBAL
ADVENTURE OR POLITICAL
ACHIEVEMENT COULD
EVER DO!

WHAT GREAT LEADERS UNDERSTAND

THEY UNDERSTAND THE IMPORTANCE OF GOALS

Leaders are goal orientated. They have short term, medium term and long term goals. Those goals can be very quantitative in terms of financial goals, sales, market share and profitability etc. And the goals can also be very qualitative in terms of brand awareness, improved organisational culture, and personal development.

The leader will ensure that, within the environment that they lead, everyone is aware of those goals, has been involved in setting those goals, and understands the road map as to how those goals are going to be achieved. Everyone will know how they contribute to achieving those goals and they will understand how their own activity, targets and objectives fit into the overall picture of achieving those goals.

THEY UNDERSTAND THE ISSUE IN THE ROOM

This is the essence of great leadership! Many fail to grasp the *issue in the room* – so let me explain.

I will give you an example. Let's say you have a sales executive underperforming in your organisation. Obviously you want to turn this around. So you bring them into the office and you investigate. Their response is that they are too busy with administrative tasks consuming their day-to-day activity, and they are thus unable to do sales calls or follow up on leads. You now have a choice. Believe them and start to implement a costly programme of decoupling the administration element of their role by employing an administrator or risk causing negativity in the office by dumping administrative tasks on to other staff. Or you don't believe them, and you instinctively know that the admin tasks equate to say five hours a week and there is no reason why they can't perform better on sales. They are either organisationally all over the place and using admin overload as a cover for their underperformance, or in reality are account administrators rather than sales people. Either way, you see past the narrative and excuses that people can so often come out with, and you fundamentally and instinctively understand the *issue in the room*. You know what is happening in reality. You are not clouded by emotions, you don't get caught up in the personalities, you are not so naive and gullible (though people may stupidly think you are) to believe everything that is coming out of people's mouths. No, you are objective, calculated and clever. You see the big picture, what is actually happening, and what is really going on. You see the **issue in the room**.

- **Sceptical eye**

  Look, you can't disbelieve everything people say. There has to be an acceptance of much of the stuff people are doing or saying. However, always have a sceptical eye. In other words, you are open to the fact that what you see and hear may not be the truth, the whole truth and nothing but the truth. Have that sceptical eye that enables you to think: "This may not be true"; "He is not as good as he or others think"; "The reason that she is giving may not be the real reason" and so on. Great leaders have a sceptical eye.

- **Decide on data**

  Your decisions on who is right or wrong, or what action needs to be taken should be based on good raw data. Not "He said, she said" stuff but real, solid, good data. Your ability to know the issue in the room will come from your understanding of what is actually going on, and that in turn will come from the data that you have sourced, read and understood. That data could be financial data, sales data, or data that you put together specifically to test the assertions that people are making.

- **Broad picture**

  Seeing the issue in the room can only be done by someone who takes a few steps back and sees the complete picture. Many people zero in on the particular problem at hand, let everything get clouded, immerse themselves in the emotion and politics of it all, become completely unable to be objective or detached, and therefore judgement and discernment goes out the window! Great leaders take a step back, stay detached, look at the bigger picture and actually see the reality of what is going on - the issue in the room.

THEY UNDERSTAND THE POWER OF THE TONGUE

The tongue is a powerful weapon. It can do a lot of damage to you and others and it can also be a force for good. So here are some pointers on one of the most powerful weapons in the world – the tongue.

- **Spheres of influence**

  Remember as you are speaking to someone, that nothing is "off record!" You can trust people if you like, but remember as my mum always says: "No matter how confidential someone says they will be, they will always tell at least one person!"

- **Speak with authority**

  You are, at the end of the day, the boss. So speak with authority. To do that you need to speak with conviction. And to speak with conviction you need to be firm on what you believe. Have strong beliefs, understand why you believe whatever you believe then speak with conviction.

- **Don't gossip**

  Don't talk about others to others. You are the one supposed to be above office politics! Any issues around competency, training, development, need to be discussed - but with the right people. In other words, discuss with those specific people or their line manager and that's it!

- **Talk shop but also ask about their dog**

  It's an organisation that is being run so many discussions will naturally be about internal matters. However, it is also important that you come alongside people, get to know them and build relationships. Be cautious on this as you will gel with some more than others, but you are at the end of the day - human.

LEADERS HAVE AN UNDERLYING MOTIVATION TO MAKE THEM GREATER

Best advice I can give to my competitors... leave me be! And if you do, I will become flabby and lazy, distracted and even bored. Attack me and push me against the ropes and that's when I am at my best. I need a war to be effective. I need a fight to win. I need to be the underdog getting a pounding from the heavyweight champion of the world. And then that's when I am dangerous. In every realm where I lead, if it is mundane and if there is no challenger and no battle then I become bored, useless, bored and I descend into a dangerous spiral of indifference and - did I mention - boredom. I remember for months going through the daily grind with no action in an organisation I worked for. One day the competitor attacked fairly aggressively, and within 24 hours I had taken four of their customers. I went on a relentless assault of market share land-grab that thrust the company to double digit growth, to become a leader in the sector. Maybe that sounds a bit perverse but for me that's what motivates. I remember when I was young playing about with a group of friends in one of my father's business colleague's large National Trust like gardens. We approached a bee hive and stupidly, really stupidly, I kicked it. I don't think I ever ran faster in my life as a swarm of bees pursued me. That kick and the consequences of it motivated me for action! A kick of the bee hive is sometimes all it takes to get motivated. Being attacked and kicked is my motivator... my red flag. What is yours? And the life lesson from the bee hive story is confirmed by something I heard from the famous BBC character Del Boy, from the TV show *Only Fools & Horses* –

"Sometimes if you stick your head in a bee hive you will get more than a nose full of honey!"

LEADERS UNDERSTAND THEY NEED TO BE LED

Who is leading you? Who is holding you to account and challenging you to be the leader you need to be? Without a challenge and accountability function in your life then you will slide more often than not to dysfunctional leadership. It is inevitable. Human nature dictates it. All of us, no matter who we are or how good we think we are, we need someone to bring us back to earth, question our motives, and make sure we are acting as leaders.

This challenge and accountability function may already

be in place in your world, and if so just make sure that the challenge is primarily around your leadership journey. The person best placed to do this is a mentor that you meet, say, every two months for lunch or coffee to challenge you and hold you to account. Buy them lunch, give them the "Start to Lead" book and say: "Question me on that!"

THEY UNDERSTAND THEMSELVES... SELF AWARENESS

Self awareness is a trait of great leadership and therefore you need to be aware of those leadership shortcomings that need to be addressed in your own life. You may not be great at communicating with a certain layer of management, you may fail to have those difficult conversations and so end up with a "head in the sand" response. You need to be comfortable with your weaknesses in finance or operations and surround yourself with people better than you in those areas, but you must never as a leader be comfortable with your specific shortcomings that are essential for leadership. For example, if you lack humility, then you shouldn't be comfortable with that. If you lack a desire to delegate or empower others you should not be comfortable with that either, as those shortcomings are failures in leadership. These shortcomings are specific leadership weaknesses that must be addressed if you are to be defined as a great leader.

SELF AWARENESS IS
A TRAIT OF GREAT
LEADERSHIP AND
THEREFORE YOU NEED
TO BE AWARE OF
THOSE LEADERSHIP
SHORTCOMINGS THAT NEED
TO BE ADDRESSED IN YOUR
OWN LIFE.

LEADERS KNOW HOW TO WORK ON WHAT NEEDS ADDRESSING

Reflect on those areas that you are not good at and start to make conscious efforts to address them by yourself or with your mentor. Therefore, if you struggle to delegate then make one act of delegation this week... just one. If you struggle with micro managing, then be brutally honest with the individual or individuals that you find yourself micro managing. Explain why you micro mange them and your fears and concerns, and then work together as a team on how you can all get to a point where fears are removed, systems are put in place, and the situation no longer requires micro managing. They will respect you for it. Also, there is a place for a bit of training, a bit of reading, and a bit of observation on how other people deal with their shortcomings. But only a bit!

LEADERS UNDERSTAND DYSFUNCTIONAL LEADERSHIP

This is the situation when a leader starts acting like a "You know what"...

Human nature, (and I have thousands of years to back this up), is and will always be imperfect. Our nature is such that we make mistakes, do not think, or act and behave as we should. So we can read books, follow a particular faith or ideology, but we will always fall short of the standard. And in leadership, we can listen, learn, and read, and try to adhere to the right course of action, but our nature will always get us in the end and take us off the rails.

Dysfunctional leadership happens when you do the

opposite of what a great leader should be doing. So you manage rather than lead, are closed rather than open, ethical rather than unethical, and so on. Dysfunctional leadership will lead to downward spirals and the impacts could be staff morale, sales, financials... the list is endless. If you are a great leader you will care, so dysfunctional patterns in leadership need to be addressed and stopped.

LEADERS KNOW THE DANGERS OF THEIR DARK SIDE

We all have a dark side. It's that one thing in our life that we should not be doing – and we know it. It is that weakness that needs dealing with otherwise it could be destructive to yourself or others. Whatever it is, as you read this, you will know what it is. If you don't know you are probably a psychopath. However, the question is what is that dark side doing to your leadership? In some perverse way it may, in the short term, help you lead and propel you forward. For example, the guilt of an unforgiving spirit to others in the past may make you a more forgiving leader. Your dark side is your thorn in the flesh... something that is, for now, part of you. The best response to that area is to mortify it, aim to conquer it, and get it out of your life.

LEADERS UNDERSTAND THAT SOME PEOPLE ARE NOT GOOD

Yes, some people are just not good. Not everyone – but some. Not everyone is redeemable, not everyone can be turned. Some people are just bad... some people are just incompetent... some people are trouble. Leaders beware. Get them out of your environment. That's your role, you must protect everyone else and protect unity and protect the quality of your organisation. So the stupid ones – get rid.

LEADERS KNOW HOW TO DEAL WITH POPULARITY

Leaders can be popular because they can massively impact on people's lives in a positive way. You are like a medieval king dispensing patronage of titles, money and gifts. You are able to bring them into your inner circle and reward them for loyalty and maybe give them wealth. So yes, you will be popular amongst those beneficiaries, and also with those who just like what you do, have done, and are doing in the world. Popularity is good, as being universally hated is hardly a great recommendation! But popularity can have its problems! It can lead to pride and pride breeds arrogance, arrogance breeds complacency, complacency breeds egotistical behaviour and then egotistical behaviour leads to downfall!

Great leaders don't let popularity go to their heads or assume that everything that they do will turn to gold. Great leaders recognise that people are fickle and popularity can go as quickly as it comes. Great leaders don't really let popularity affect them at all – because they see it for what it is.

LEADERS UNDERSTAND RELATIONSHIPS

Relationship building with those around you is part of the leadership's role. However, leaders understand people and they understand relationships. They build relationships with wise and experienced individuals who perhaps become their unofficial mentors. They build relationships with staff but know the reality of the enemy within an organisation and those people who are dangerous and bad news and those who are positive for you and the organisation as a whole. Great leaders understand the nature of the relationship that should be formed with particular individuals. Some you keep at a distance and some you can bring into your inner circle, some you trust (to a point) and others you don't.

THEY SEE BOTH ALLIES AND ENEMIES

There are those, both within your environment and outside it, who will be your allies. They will work with you, be friends with you, and have a great working relationship with you. Allies have your back covered and they are on "your side of the desk." Allies will make sacrifices for you and they will defend you, support you, encourage you, and help you. And yes, as there are allies there are also enemies. Enemies in short are the opposite of allies, and will act accordingly. In leadership, your world will have both. Be comfortable with that, be prepared for that, and understand how to deal with it.

THEY UNDERSTAND THE LONELINESS OF LEADERSHIP

There is the old saying, "It's lonely at the top." Yeah it is lonely, but fortunately I like it that way because I am essentially a loner. So I am very happy! For many though they don't like it that way. In leadership friendships are few and enemies may be many. Not everyone can cope with this but hey, as I said before, there are very few people who are true leaders. However, in leadership, a sense of loneliness can lead to depression; it can lead to cynicism, and a general antipathy towards others. None of these things are healthy. So if you feel lonely, try to get out more and make friends. Obvious, but it is worth doing!

LEADERS KNOW THAT BEHIND EVERY GREAT LEADER...

Behind every good leader is a wife, a husband, a partner, a father, a mother, a family member or a friend. There is someone behind every leader. That person is hurting when they hurt, rejoicing when the leader rejoices, holding them up, and keeping them grounded. Behind every great leader is the unknown leader, the leader of that leader. That person is the unofficial mentor, the life coach, the shoulder to cry on. They are the unsung heroes, the ones who rarely get any air time and who probably get no consideration or credit from others. However, all leaders owe them a great deal.

As a leader, you need to make sure that such mentors know they are appreciated, and loved, and that you recognise all they do for you. Reciprocate and do what you can to tangibly show your appreciation.

SUCCESS HAS MANY PARENTS... FAILURES ARE QUICKLY ORPHANED.

Success tends to attract attention, support, a following, a jumping on the band wagon, or a holding on of shirt tails. Success brings popularity, friends, and plenty of people queuing up to get on the bus, and join the ride. Leaders understand that success brings all of these things and indeed has many parents, real and imagined.

However, great leaders do not get too high on it because

they know that they are "one trade away from humility", and that it can all go terribly wrong. And with failure (yes there is such a thing), all of the success gains can disappear and people will jump ship, detach themselves and distance themselves right quick. Failures are, sadly but inevitably, quickly orphaned. Great leaders understand this reality and the really great ones are comfortable with it.

THERE IS A TIME TO EXIT THE STAGE

My father-in-law was a pastor for most of his life. When he first got into the ministry he put a circle around the date of his retirement. He knew when he would be exiting the stage and all great leaders should at least be working towards that exit (even though they may not actually circle the date!).

A DAY IN THE LIFE OF A LEADER

THE DAY STARTS WITH THE MINDSET

Leaders are human. They wake up and get up like everyone else. However, what makes someone a great leader is what is going on in their heads. The leader has in their mindset that they are going to walk into that group of people at 9.00 am and help them achieve goals by encouraging them, helping them, and doing whatever they can do to make that environment a place where goals can be achieved and, in doing so, make the world just that little bit better for the people and organisation they lead.

IT'S ALL ABOUT THE GOALS

Leaders will have those short term, medium term and long term goals rattling around in their heads. They will be making sure that everyone is aware of those goals by communicating them, reinforcing them, promoting them and holding people to account – and making sure others do the same. Leaders will be making sure that people's activity, work, and personal goals are all aligned with the overall goals of the organisation. Goal alignment is crucial in leading people.

Great leaders then continue throughout the day making great decisions. Life is full of decision making, we do it every day. Some of those decisions have limited impact, other decisions we make can have a significant influence on the environment we operate in. We make small decisions concerning the paint on the office wall, and the positioning of the photocopier (sorry these things may be big to some), and other times we make significant decisions like the contracts we secure, the investments we make, the people we hire, the promotions we give, and the systems that we implement.

Great leaders create an environment that enables great decisions to be made by everyone. Most of us have a tendency to base our decisions on assumptions, anecdotal evidence, or perhaps emotive reasons. However, great leaders love data when it comes to making decisions. It isn't personalities, emotions and feelings that guide a leader; it is good solid facts based on concrete data. When decisions need to be made, the great leaders base it on data. It should not typically be on gut instinct or any of the other entrepreneurial clichés. For example, a decision to enter a new market should be based on thorough research and analysis rather than a "Let's go for it!" mentality.

LEADERS WILL HAVE THOSE
SHORT TERM, MEDIUM
TERM AND LONG TERM
GOALS RATTLING AROUND
IN THEIR HEADS. THEY WILL
BE MAKING SURE THAT
EVERYONE IS AWARE OF THOSE
GOALS BY COMMUNICATING
THEM, REINFORCING THEM,
PROMOTING THEM AND
HOLDING PEOPLE TO ACCOUNT
ON THEM – AND MAKING SURE
OTHERS DO THE SAME.

Therefore, in creating that environment that enables goals to be achieved, decisions must be based on reality – good solid facts based on reliable data. The problem with data is that it is everywhere! To avoid data overload it is important to do the following:

- **Determine the key performance indicators you need:**

  What are the key performance indicators that you need to determine the health of your environment and whether goals will be achieved? If you are leading sales, the data needed may be conversion rates, profit per sales rep, sales growth and so on. Or if you are heading up operations, the data needed may be key numbers around labour costs, staff turnover, and productivity.

- **Get the data**

  You need to make sure you have the right data that will give you all the information you need to make that informed right decision. Wrong data then wrong decision. Make sure the key data holders are brought together, tell them the decisions that need to be made and make sure that there is consensus on whether the data they have is in fact relevant to your needs.

  Determine those key numbers that really matter and the data that you require to give you those numbers reliably and regularly. The data is probably there, but work out a way to ensure that the data is accurate and easily accessible and presentable. As a leader it is not your job to search through endless documents trying to make sense of it all. The data needs to be pulled together, analysed, and presented in a way that makes sense and that can enable you to make the informed decisions that will enable goals to be achieved. Get your IT department/service company to make sure your systems can use the data to generate the right reports and that the report generation and analysis is easy and quick! Make sure you make it clear to the ones who are putting the data capture, analysis and reporting systems together what information you want, how it needs to be presented and why you want it. I don't know why IT people want to know the "why", they just do... they always do!

- **Make sure the data is relevant and stays relevant**

  You will need to continually evaluate whether the data that you have and base decisions on is still relevant. There may be Key Performance Indicators that you had five years ago that simply may no longer be relevant. Information may be nice to see, capture and read, but does it help you make decisions? Make sure that the KPIs, reports and information you receive are still relevant by reviewing on an annual basis. And the relevancy test is simple – does it help you make decisions to enable your goals to be achieved? Simple! You really don't want a situation where someone is spending a lot of their time producing weekly reports that nobody reads or make decisions with because it lacks relevance.

- **Make the right decision and implement it**

  People hate it when commitments are given but not kept, when promises are not delivered, and when the decisions made in a meeting are not implemented. They detest it! It hits morale and the leader looks like an ass - an indecisive, incompetent fool who can't get their act together and never has either the guts or the basic organisational skills to actually implement the decisions needing to be made. So make sure you do what you say you are going to do – make the decision and implement it.

Now, having said all that, sometimes we will make unwise decisions and say silly stuff that gets people's backs up, and we will think to ourselves – "That was stupid of me to say that." Don't worry, don't sweat it – everyone says and does stupid things at times.

LEADERS SWEAT THEIR MOST VALUABLE ASSET... INFORMATION

Information is everything. If you want to lead - then you need information. And I'm not talking secondary information that you can pick up on any search engine! The information I am talking about is information that is *primary*. It isn't available at the click of a button. This information is rich, it's possibly strategic and it has the potential to give you, your people, and your organisation an edge that enables those goals to be achieved that you have set.

There are a number of ways that you can get this type of valuable information:

• **Hang out with other leaders**

Leaders tend to flock together and play in the same sand boxes so make sure you are cultivating relationships with players and people of influence that are actually making decisions at many different levels of society. Obvious point!

- **Attend specific industry events**

  My business partner, James, and I run an on-site shredding business called ShredBank, and there actually is a shredding association annual event that we attend! Whatever industry you are in then attend their industry specific events. And don't just mingle - form relationships, get into conversations, do dinner dates and follow up.

- **Be intellectually curious**

  Always be in learning mode. Every time you get into a conversation inquire about the other person, their industry (whatever industry they are in), their business, how it functions, what makes it successful, and how it performs. Be intellectually curious about the way the world works and nuggets of rich information will come your way.

- **Observe the world around you**

  Few people do this. Look around, lift some stones, keep watching what others are doing, always be listening, always be looking, keep reading and keep observing.

LEADERS DESTROY OR DELEGATE

A leader should be doing two things when it comes to files and paperwork – destroy or delegate. The information that you have all around you is either important or it is not. It either needs to be kept for operational or legal reasons or it is no longer relevant and can be destroyed. OK, personal confession, as I mentioned I co-own ShredBank, a shredding business, with my friend and business partner James so I have a vested interested in promoting the virtues of destroying unnecessary paperwork - but the point is still valid. Quite simply - if you don't need it then destroy it! If you do need the documents, then try to delegate the administrative, financial or operational duties and tasks that apply to those documents.

LEADERS ENCOURAGE

You should make a point of encouraging people. Be interested in what they do both in and outside of work (if the door opens and they volunteer that), and encourage them on their journey. Everyone needs to be appreciated, listened to, supported, helped, and valued. And if you make people feel this way you will encourage them. A great leader encourages. Encouraging energises people; they feel more positive about themselves and the environment that they are in. Should I really be extolling the benefits of encouraging people? I'll stop right now – you get the picture – it is the right thing to do! Oh, and remember this quote when determining who you will encourage and help on their journey:

"You can easily judge the character of a man by how he treats those who can do nothing for him."

Malcolm S. Forbes.

YOU SHOULD MAKE A POINT
OF ENCOURAGING PEOPLE. BE
INTERESTED IN WHAT THEY
DO BOTH IN AND OUTSIDE OF
WORK (IF THE DOOR OPENS AND
THEY VOLUNTEER THAT), AND
ENCOURAGE THEM ON THEIR
JOURNEY.

I have a tendency to be excessive and that's why I don't drink alcohol. If I did drink alcohol and I liked it, I would do to alcohol what I do to chocolate - and I would end up a regular in Betty Ford Clinic. For me, unfortunately I have no hobbies, so business is my hobby - it's my sand box. I am like a kid in a sweet shop when it comes to business, playing around merrily while adults look on with disdain. However, it is much better to get a hobby.

LEADERS STICK TO THE PARAMETERS OF THEIR LEADERSHIP ROLE

In daily work life, great leaders are disciplined in ensuring that they stick to their "leadership brief." Great leaders therefore:

- **Don't manage...** that's for others

- **Don't get entangled...** that's for others to sort out

- **Don't get too tactical...** they are more strategic

- **Don't go to every meeting...** they are not or should not be needed

- **Don't front every initiative...** leaders need to empower others to do that

COLLECTIVE LEADERSHIP

Solo leadership is a fairly rare thing. More often than not a leader will be leading in company with other leaders. Whether you are leading with a fellow business partner or on a board of directors or a committee there are a few points I want to get across about collective leadership.

In collective leadership, when it comes to short, medium and long term goals there are a number of questions where there needs to be a positive answer:

1. Have goals been set and documented?
2. Has everyone been involved in the process of goal setting?
3. Have those goals been collectively determined and agreed?
4. Is there agreement on how those goals are to be achieved?
5. Is there agreement on who will be held accountable for certain goals?

DETERMINE WHO DOES WHAT

Each leader has something different to bring to the party. Some will be entrepreneurial; others will be more operational, and others will lean towards the administrator type of leadership role. Understand where everyone fits in the leadership picture. Everyone should be comfortable with their own contribution and the contribution that other leaders are making.

NOT EVERYONE IS YOU!

You may be a die hard, work until 12.00 am every night, downing energy drinks and turning up in the morning opening the doors to be first in the office type of leader – but you can't expect your fellow leaders to be like that. Nor should you berate them for not being like you. Everyone works at a different pace, everybody is at a different stage in their own personal life cycle. Understand that everyone is different. That doesn't mean that we should accept mediocrity; it's that we should accept diversity.

THERE SHOULD BE UNANIMITY ON DEFINING THE "LEADERSHIP ROLE"

As leaders, everyone should agree on what a leader is there to do. Everyone should be clear that leaders are there to create an environment that achieves goals... and others will manage. Get consensus on what a day to day role would look like so that everyone is comfortable with it. This will avoid potential tension and arguments because you could have a situation, for example, where one leader may be more inclined to a managerial style and may as a result be aggravated by his or her fellow leaders who are adopting true leadership styles by striving to be less hands on and more focused on creating and building an environment that achieves goals that have been set.

LEADERS ARE OVERSEERS

The leader is an overseer. A leader is not someone who gets into the weeds and manages everything to oblivion. Think of a leader as the owner of a beautiful garden. The leader will need to ensure that the environment has everything it needs, so that goals will be achieved. The leader will get the people in place - appoint perhaps a skilled gardener to cut the grass, trim the bushes, and plant the seeds. The leader will make sure the necessary infrastructure is in place such as lawn mower, garden tools, and plant feed. They will make sure that the processes are in place for when certain tasks need to be done and what resources are required to do it. And then the leader will determine that a culture of freshness, colour, tranquility, and beauty comes from all that activity. The leader sees to it that this is all happening in perfect unison. He or she will not cut the grass but they will check that it has been cut right, advise the gardener on some of their shortcomings but also encourage them on a job well done. The equipment will all need to work and be properly maintained, so the leader oversees this happening too. You are there to oversee the garden, and to put people, organisation, infrastructure and culture in place, all to ensure that it is a lush environment – the most beautiful garden in existence. You are there to lead – others will manage. So let's now look, in the next four chapters, in greater depth on the four areas that leaders must focus on – **Infrastructure, People, Organisation** and **Culture.**

YOU ARE THERE TO LEAD...
OTHERS WILL MANAGE

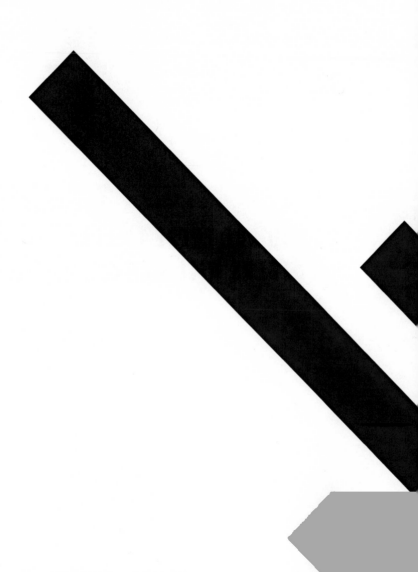

LEADERSHIP AND INFRASTRUCTURE

LEADERSHIP AND INFRASTRUCTURE

The infrastructure is about the physical and tangible aspects of the environment you lead. It can be as basic as the building with its tables and chairs, and include more complex areas such as the IT systems, software and complex machinery. Infrastructure is that part of the environment that equips people to achieve those goals that have been agreed by leadership. Infrastructure could be the machines to produce the widgets, the computers to process the information, the desks and chairs for people to work from, the stationery, the IT equipment, the tools, the trucks, the cars and so on. Leadership is not just about making sure that the infrastructure is in place to enable goals to be achieved, but that the infrastructure is maintained to continue to be relevant and reliable for the needs of whatever environment it serves.

I have worked for a number of organisations over the course of my career and, in terms of infrastructure I have seen the worst and the best. In previous employment I have had a leaky warehouse that soaked the stock if it rained hard enough, and toilets in the very same warehouse that, let's say, looked like a cow had been there many times! I have experienced computers that needed kicked to start (anyone older than 40 will remember this). I have had a smelly kitchen that I don't think anyone ever really found out where the smell was coming from despite the brave efforts of one of the cleaners. However, on the other hand I have seen the best of infrastructure. ShredBank is the best example of investment and sustained investment in infrastructure in my experience. My business partner James is an expert in the area of creating the ultimate infrastructure to enable goals to be achieved.

James's philosophy is to ensure that resources in all forms are always there in order to efficiently and effectively always deliver for the client (our goal). Our office environment has modern chair and desk units, high quality carpets and tiles, lovely fresh kitchen and restroom facilities. The office environment is one that makes staff love where they work, ensuring that everything they need to achieve goals is there for them, and that all the infrastructure crucially works and is fit for purpose, and is maintained to stay that way. As a mobile shredding company we also have the most advanced mobile shredding technology in the industry with robust maintenance programmes to ensure our fleet is reliable and efficient.

All this is said, not as an advert for ShredBank, but to underline its importance for you, as a current or future business leader, as you think about what you will aim to provide in your particular sphere.

The principles of infrastructure investment, in my experience, are as follows:

- Think long term when purchasing anything relating to infrastructure

- Go for quality every time, price is secondary more often than not

- Only purchase and use that which enables goals to be achieved

- Think how the infrastructure will support and impact on culture, people, and organisation when thinking infrastructure investment

- Maintain the infrastructure through good policies, service agreements, upgrading, etc.

- Upgrade your organisation's infrastructure when necessary (which is usually a couple of years before *you* think it is necessary)

- Keep it relevant through investment, maintenance and upgrading. Make sure you let the specialists tell you what is required, and when it is required, and listen to their advice - they probably know better than you!

- Ensure it is given both tactical and strategic focus within the organisation. It is important to achieving long term goals in the organisation.

LEADERSHIP
AND PEOPLE

BRINGING THEM IN...

It's vital to get the right people into your environment. One of my favourite films "A Man for all Seasons" has a dialogue where the King describes the type of people that he leads. The King wants Sir Thomas More to support him on a matter and Sir Thomas More asks why he needs his support. The King replies,

Because you're honest... and what is more to the purpose, you're known to be honest. There are those like Norfolk who follow me because I wear the crown, those like Master Cromwell who follow me because they are jackals with sharp teeth and I'm their tiger, there's a mass that follows me because it follows anything that moves. And then there's you.

The King's assessment of his kingdom and his followers is very bleak. Some follow because he holds the title, others for their own personal agendas, and then there are those who will follow anything that moves. Then there are people of conviction and integrity. A leader has to lead them all. Fundamentally greatness is built on the foundations of great people. Without great people, goals will not be achieved. So a great leader will want to recruit great people. At interview stage the following questions should be asked:

Interview questions:

- **"Why are you here?" Don't accept the first answer... ask again - "Okay, but why are you here?"**

  The text book *"Say what you want them to hear"* answer will come out. Reject that. It's meaningless. Ask again, to try to get to the real truthful answer as to why they are sitting in front of you. Why do they want to leave their current employment? Why do they want to come and work for you? Getting to the truth here is vital in making sure expectations are managed both for you as the leader and them as the potential employee.

- **What is your gift? What are you gifted in?**

  This question is never asked but it is crucial. Essentially you are asking the person something deeper than their key strength or key skill. You are asking them to define themselves, to open up to you as to what their ultimate offering to the world is that sets them apart. It is that natural ability that has been given to them at birth and nurtured through the experiences of life that ultimately could be used for the good of your organisation.

- **Talk to me about office politics? What are your thoughts?**

  One, do they even understand what the term means? Two, their views and opinions expressed will be crucial in how they are going to interact with other people. You want to find out what their ideological

FUNDAMENTALLY GREATNESS IS BUILT ON THE FOUNDATIONS OF GREAT PEOPLE. WITHOUT GREAT PEOPLE, GOALS WILL NOT BE ACHIEVED.

view is on it – would backstabbing, character assassination, and divisions be things that they set themselves apart from? Are they peace makers or peace breakers? Do they instinctively know how office politics works and how to deal with it?

- **Tell them the truth... the whole truth and nothing but the truth**

  Sometimes if leaders really want someone to work for them they will not be completely honest. Bad move. It is just building up problems for you in the future. If the salary is unlikely to rise above £22K then tell them. If the job promotion scope is limited then tell them. If you expect them to deliver £100K in the first three months then tell them. Tell them everything, warts and all. Be brutally honest. Will it put them off joining you? Possibly - but it saves a lot of pain and difficult conversations down the line.

- **What are your red lines?**

  They may be confused at the question but don't elaborate too much. They need to know your red lines - and you need to know theirs. They need to know what makes you tick and what ticks you off! Extended lunch breaks, using the mobile phone during working hours, not delivering agreed outputs etc. - they need to know what will prompt knuckle rapping or sacking. And in turn, you need to know what their red lines are. It may be no staff training, lack of managerial engagement, no bonuses or whatever bothers them. They need to know and you need to know!

- **Promotion triggers**

  They need to know what *good* looks like. What will get them up the corporate ladder? Lay it all out and let there be no misunderstanding. They need to know the triggers. What will trigger a pay rise, what will trigger a job promotion, what will get them recognised and in the frame for the next stage in their development. This saves any confusion or misunderstanding in the future.

- **First 100 Days**

  Many Prime Ministers and Presidents are judged initially on their first 100 days in office. What impact have they made? What changes have been put in place? What new initiatives are they driving? The first 100 days in the job is crucial. You need to know what their thoughts are in the first 100 days. What do they plan to do, and what are their outputs? Outputs may be "Integration with team", "Get to know the company and the industry", or "Sales of 1000 widgets". Whatever it is, get them to write a report on the first 100 days and deliver it to you before the second interview. This report will be highly revealing – it will give you insights into their report writing skills, communication skills, their understanding of your organisation and the job description. It will also give you an insight into their interest in integration, skills development, training, induction, and achieving key deliverables. And also, it is the document to ultimately hold them to account.

KEEPING THEM IN...

- **Build them up:** When leading people, it is important to keep them motivated, encouraged, and feeling good about themselves. To do this you need to lift them up at times by recognising them for what they do, by inspiring them, and encouraging them. However, you are also there to lift them up in terms of their career development, their leadership potential, their remuneration, their rewards and whatever else you believe is relevant.

- **Build variety:** Mix it up for people in order that they don't stagnate. Ensure that people are constantly up skilling and learning new things. Think multi-skilling and multi-tasking in order to build an environment that is resilient to changes in personnel but also ensure they are developing themselves as individuals. There should be variety in people's roles, so encourage job swapping and opportunities to work cross functionally with other people, teams or divisions. All of this will keep the organisation fresh and invigorated.

- **Build goals:** Everyone needs goals. They need targets and something to aim for and strive towards.

Without goals people are directionless and become de-motivated. The leader must make people aware of key goals within the organisation, why those goals have been set and their role and contribution in achieving those goals. They need to have a sense of ownership of the goals and believe that they are possible. If they have no faith – it's finished! Therefore, leadership must make sure people have *personal* goals, targets and objectives that are aligned with the overall goals being set.

- **Build trust:** Build trust with everyone. And to build trust, just be honest in your dealings. If you have done something wrong – admit it – no shame in that. Be open and transparent. Deliver on what you have promised and if you can't, then apologise and explain why. Always make sure you are true and honest in how you deal with others and then actively promote a culture of trust in your environment that you are leading. An environment of mistrust is poisonous and divisive and can lead to an organisation being pulled apart. It is to be avoided. However, you must take the lead. Build trust and others will follow your lead.

- **Build understanding:** Those you lead are, at the end of the day, people. They are human. They have worries, fears, hopes, and they have weaknesses and strengths. They have a past and a present and they have a future. They may have difficulties at home, relationship problems, or health worries. Try to understand that the people you lead are going through all sorts of issues in their life. So try to understand this a little bit before you react to something they have done or haven't done. And just remember what my mum always says when I moan about one person or another - *"Be easy on them because you just don't know what they are going through."*

- **Build a leadership environment:** Leaders delegate, and encourage others to do the same. Leaders empower others to do great things, and encourage others to do the same. Leaders work laterally, and encourage others to do the same. Leaders are self aware, and encourage others to be the same. Leaders encourage, help and enable - and encourage others to do the same. Leaders lead, and... encourage others to do the same.

PUSH, PROD AND PROTECT

- **Push:** Push people, as they have great potential. Sometimes people need a gentle push to achieve great things, sometimes they need a big push and other times they need to be rammed like a wrecking ball!

- **Prod:** As I sat one day feeling a bit vulnerable to the constant barrage of unrealistic expectations of my boss and being metaphorically slapped for not meeting them, my PA give me the explanation. "He's just prodding you Phil, he is just trying to see how you react, test you and get the best out of you." Sometimes as a leader we need to prod and be prodded ourselves even though it can be painful and annoying!

- **Protect:** The leader is there to protect people in terms of their careers, their livelihoods, their development, and even their emotional and mental well-being. A leader must have a true sense of being the protector of those they lead.

PUSH PEOPLE, AS THEY HAVE GREAT POTENTIAL. SOMETIMES PEOPLE NEED A GENTLE PUSH TO ACHIEVE GREAT THINGS, SOMETIMES THEY NEED A BIG PUSH AND OTHER TIMES THEY NEED TO BE RAMMED LIKE A WRECKING BALL!

LEADING DEFINITELY WILLS, DEFINITELY MIGHTS & DEFINITELY WON'TS!

Great leaders understand that some people are just awkward. They will just not do something because they don't want to please you. You know the type of person. If you told them to look up they would look down.

We once organised a corporate hospitality event for a number of clients. We asked twenty one people to attend a wonderful dinner event at a great restaurant. No pressure, just *come and eat* was the pitch. They all agreed to come to the event. On the day of the corporate hospitality event, only seven people turned up! A business colleague of mine (invited to the event) who had a lot of wisdom and experience of running events over the years explained what had happened as I munched my chicken and potatoes with rent-a-crowd around me to make the numbers look better! She basically told me the following which I think is great advice.

Essentially there are three types of people when anyone agrees to do something. There are those who will agree to something, and come hail, rain or shine they will turn up because they agreed to do it. They will be there and that is absolute. Then there will be those who agree to do it, intend to do it, but it only takes a bit of rain or hail to put them off. They will not do what they agreed to do for what they believe is fairly justifiable reasons. They might be there, but that is not certain. Then there are those who agree to do it, but have no intention of doing it... ever! The reasons for agreeing but not intending to do it – I have no idea – ask a psychologist! The main thing we need to know is that these people exist – and there are a lot of them. They are on boards, in the work place, in organisations, in families - they are everywhere!

Therefore, for example, if you ever organise an event and want twenty-one people to attend, you should actually invite at least forty to guarantee a reasonable show of people because if twenty-one people say they will be there I can guarantee you that seven will definitely turn up, seven might turn up (if the sun is shining and the wind is blowing in the right direction), and seven will definitely not turn up! Get to know and discern who are the "definitely wills", "definitely mights" and "definitely won'ts" in the environment you lead!

LEADING UNDERPERFORMERS

Leading great people is great for you and everyone else. Leading good people is pretty good. Leading OK people is just OK. Leading underperformers is terrible. Some people are redeemable and they can be developed and worked with. A leader needs to judge whether this timely and costly process is worth it. However, underperformance can't be tolerated for too long. All leaders know the implications of keeping the wrong people in an environment that is trying to achieve challenging goals. Therefore, work on underperformers if you see a light somewhere – otherwise get rid of them!

THREE DOGS... SOMETIMES IT JUST ISN'T WORKING

When I was young my family had a dog - it was a black retriever. His name was Tufty. Unfortunately, Tufty got shot by a farmer who thought he was going for his sheep. Tufty would hold my guinea pig in his mouth and didn't harm him, so I think the farmer was a bit too trigger happy that day. Then we got another dog, and that dog caught his collar by accident on the latch of the dog pen we kept him in at night. He hung himself and sadly he died. Then the third dog, well, he just plain ran away.

The rather crude family joke was that he must have heard about the previous two dogs and decided to move. True story and the moral of this story is that perhaps the Bain family is better not having a dog. Three goes and maybe we should have read the signs and accepted the reality that maybe... just maybe we aren't good dog keepers.

Sometimes if something or someone doesn't work after one... two... or three times then maybe, just maybe, it is never going to work. Don't grip on to what maybe is a bad thing for too long... consider ditching something or someone if it doesn't work.

GETTING THEM OUT

Sometimes people are just plain wrong for your organisation. Get them out. It's as straightforward as that. There are of course those that if you spend some time and money and energy you will get them back on track. That should be the first approach to someone who appears to be the wrong fit for your environment. However, for those who are clearly not right - get rid.

LEADING PEOPLE IN COMPLEX ENVIRONMENTS

Leaders sometimes have to deal with highly complex environments. That may be heading up a department of software geniuses, dealing with your first acquisition, or running a department where nearly everything they say doesn't seem to make any sense.

As a General Manager a number of years ago, I made an acquisition of a company to complement the activities of the organisation. It was a complex business. I had become the leader of this new *bolt on* division but I didn't know anything about the business. I initially thought you needed to be a technical genius to run it, and I certainly wasn't that! In addition, the business had huge problems. There was poor morale, terrible management, tears and tantrums, and daily quality issues. It was a mess and I had no clue how to fix it or as a leader what value I could add. The issue was technical and complex, and if I could understand that complex problem then everything might fall into place. The difficulty was that I didn't understand the technical and process related problems - never mind the solution to them. So did that mean I couldn't lead? No. If it needed anything it needed leadership. Remember, the leader is not there to manage but to create an environment to enable goals to be achieved. So, like everything, it starts with people. As the leader I needed to get this sorted but it didn't require me to understand the technicalities of the software or the complex processes. I just needed to understand that it wasn't working and I needed to use leadership to fix it. So here is what I did.

BRING CALM

First, my door was wide open for people to come in and cry, pour their hearts out, and talk it out. I was there to empathise, encourage and advise around the general office issues that we all faced.

FIND THE ADULT IN THE ROOM

In any team there is someone who is behaving more maturely than others. He or she may not necessarily be the complete solution but in times of trying to find solutions you need to talk to "Adults" to bring a reasoned, logical and unemotional assessment of what is going on. I found that Adult. He gave me that assessment.

FIND THE EXPERT WHO CAN SORT OUT THE COMPLEXITY

There will be someone sitting there who has the technical brains to sort it. Now that person may have been wrongly overlooked or marginalised because they lack interpersonal skills, they maybe are difficult to work with or they haven't been listened to. So I found the Expert. He was on his final written warning.

EXPERT AND ADULT COMBO

Get the Adult and elevate him by formalising the role he or she was informally doing. Bring the Expert out from the cold. Bring them together and facilitate the journey of complexity to simplicity, disorganisation to organisation, and problems to solutions.

Oversee their progress and show them what they need to deliver. Encourage and motivate. Bonuses, lunches, and pay rises may be needed. Invest in infrastructure if they need it, give them training, and buddy/mentor them. And finally, set up some key goals around financials, outputs, and performance, to hold them to account.

You may think that all seems easy. You may be thinking - leadership is a handy number if that is all a leader does. Well, few people can do it. Firstly, spotting an Adult is difficult if you are not one. Not everyone behaves like an Adult. Secondly, leaders are people who others want to follow. If you don't act, talk and behave like a leader the Adult won't want to follow. Thirdly, most will either run away in fear from the difficult and complex problems, but only leaders will have the courage and mental and emotional stamina to sort the problem out. Fourthly, some will want to stick their nose in and potentially make the situation worse by managing the problem themselves. A leader will know they can't personally manage it but will look for a man or woman who can! Fifthly, most will have sacked the Expert, only a leader can see past his weaknesses in an unemotional detached manner and embrace the Expert as the saviour. Sixthly, only a leader has the power, the levers and the energy to recreate the environment to enable goals to be achieved.

DEVELOPING FUTURE LEADERS

As a leader you need to be about developing leaders all the time, and here are a few things to consider:

- **You have to see something**

  Before you start them on the journey of leadership you need to see if it is in them to begin with. If there is not something there, then you can't develop them into leaders.

- **Have they got what it takes?**

  Are they showing the traits and characteristics of leadership? Are they creating environments to enable goals to be achieved, are they showing humility, doing great things, adding value, being last out, and showing ownership?

- **Are they already doing it?**

  You need to spot random acts of leadership where

they are enabling goals to be achieved. Look to see if they are informally fulfilling a leadership role.

- **Learning to ride a bike**

  Don't just stick them on the bike and expect them to do wheelies and cycle like a pro for the first time. They will need the stabilisers on for a while, they will need supported and cushioned, hand held, protected in order to get to the point where they can ride that leadership journey without the same level of adult supervision.

- **Mentor them**

  Make sure you mentor them specifically on the art of leadership. They need to be challenged to think, act, talk, and walk like a leader.

- **Throw them a few small leadership tasks**

  Give them some small leadership tasks and see how they get on. Give them tasks and key goals and observe how they go about it, what is the impact, and how people take to their act of leadership.

- **Then some big tasks**

  If they knocked the small leadership tasks out of the park and achieved goals then give them some chunky tasks to really test them. Give them something substantive that involves infrastructure, people, organisation and culture.

BUT FOR SOME PEOPLE... AVOID LEADERSHIP... "BE A TEACHER."

There are some who want leadership for all the wrong reasons. They want it for prestige, for affirmation, for popularity, for control, or perhaps the deep desire to just plain manage people and tell them what to do – to make them (the wannabe leader) feel good! There are those who want to be in leadership because it is developmental, the next stage in their career. There are those who want to be a leader because it may appear sexy and interesting. There are those who want it for the status, for the kudos and for the recognition.

These are all the wrong reasons, and if the above describes you then stay away from it, as you will most likely be a bad leader and cause grief to others. As I mentioned earlier, one of my all-time favourite films was called a "Man for All Seasons". The film's story is set between 1529 and 1535, at the high point of the reign of King Henry VIII of England. The main character, Sir Thomas More, was the 16th-century Lord Chancellor of England who refused to sign a letter asking Pope Clement VII to annul Henry VIII's marriage to Catherine of Aragon and he then resigned rather than take an Oath of

Supremacy declaring Henry VIII Supreme Head of the Church of England. Whatever the rights or wrongs, More was a highly respected character in leadership who took a principled stand and faced the ultimate consequence of doing so – death.

In one early scene in the film, there is a character called Richard Rich who is an ambitious young man drawn to political power and leadership, wants the trappings and prestige associated with it, and as can be seen from the rest of the film - will do whatever it takes to get it. However, in the early part of the film, Richard Rich pleads with More for a prominent leadership position at Court. The dialogue goes like this:

"*Thomas More: Have you been here all night?*
Richard Rich: Yes. You said there was a post?
Thomas More: Yes. I'll offer you a post with a house, a servant and fifty pounds a year
Richard Rich: What post?
Thomas More: At the new school.
Richard Rich: A teacher!
Thomas More: Richard, no one's going to give you a place at court.
Richard Rich: Master Cromwell says he'll do something for me.
Thomas More: Cromwell? Well, if you know Cromwell, you don't need my help.
Richard Rich: Sir Thomas? If only you knew how much... much rather, I had your help than his.
Thomas More: Not to a place at court.
Richard Rich: Why not?
Thomas More: Look! (showing the silver chalice).
Richard Rich: What is it?

Thomas More: It's a bribe! "I am the gift of Averil Machin." And Averil Machin has a lawsuit in the Court of Requests. Italian Silver. Take it! No joke.

Richard Rich: Thank you.

Thomas More: What will you do with it?

Richard Rich: Sell it.

Thomas More: And buy what?

Richard Rich: A decent gown!

Thomas More: But Richard, that's a little bribe. At court they offer you all sorts of things, home, manor houses, coats of arms. A man should go where he won't be tempted. Why not be a teacher? You'd be a fine teacher. Perhaps a great one.

Richard Rich: If I was, who would know it?

Thomas More: You! Your pupils. Your friends. God. Not a bad public, that. And a quiet life.

Richard Rich: You say that. You come from talking with the Cardinal.

Thomas More: Yes, talking with the Cardinal. It's eating your heart out, isn't it? The high affairs of state…. be a teacher."

If you are pursuing leadership for all the wrong reasons, take More's advice – do something else! Be a teacher… a fine teacher… perhaps even a great one.

IF YOU ARE PURSUING LEADERSHIP FOR ALL THE WRONG REASONS, TAKE MORE'S ADVICE – DO SOMETHING ELSE! BE A TEACHER... A FINE TEACHER... PERHAPS EVEN A GREAT ONE.

HAVE A RETENTION STRATEGY?

Personally I think a "retention strategy" is a waste of time. Do all the right things and people might stay or they might not. In the final analysis, people leave and people stay for all sorts of reasons which can largely be out of your control. We live, as we all know, in a fluid world of constant change and a retention strategy is pointless. In light of this, create an environment that ensures that you are not dependent on anyone and essentially, everyone is expendable (including you). There! No need to worry about a retention strategy.

LEADERSHIP AND ORGANISATION

ORGANISATIONAL JOURNEY

A number of years ago, I was speaking to a friend of mine who runs a significant legal practice that had a large corporate client base. It was during the recession, and many companies were closing down and really struggling. I asked him how his legal practice was performing under such difficult economic circumstances His answer made me smile. He said, "We are going great, Phil, because we get them on the way up, and we get them on the way down!" A bit harsh but it is the reality of many organisations. There are certain things that are inevitable in life. And one of those inevitabilities is the organisational journey. Organisations have a starting point, they are born, they grow, they push to the top of what their capabilities and market allow them and then, if the right interventions are not made, they slide into decline and potential irrelevancy. Leaders could find themselves leading at any stage in the organisational journey, and if you are to lead effectively, you need to understand what is happening to your organisation at whatever stage in the journey it finds itself.

LEADING "ON THE WAY UP"

You may have to lead an organisation that is just off the starting blocks. And inevitably this requires the leader to be more entrepreneurial. Leadership at this stage is about being very commercially focused, creative, innovative and with a willingness to take risks. Without an entrepreneurial style of leadership the start-up organisation will just burn out. And in fact, in the future, if entrepreneurial leadership leaves the building individually and culturally then the organisation will descend into decline and irrelevancy because there will not be the creativity and innovation necessary to adapt to change. The leader's concern at this stage is about two things – sales and cash. There are no complex organisational structures – it's all very simple. If you get enough sales and customers, and break through the sustainable barrier you will start to grow. You will become a movement! And as you move up, you are adding customers, building market share and more people are joining the movement as either employees or as customers. Sales, profitability, and growth are becoming the order of the day.

However, when your business grows, you have to *grow up*, in terms of building in good organisational structures, systems and processes to make certain that everything operates efficiently and effectively. As things develop, leadership needs to be still entrepreneurial, but must see to it that it includes more operationally focused leadership in the environment, so that things can actually get done efficiently and effectively and the customer is always getting what has been promised. Entrepreneurial leaders have a tendency to be more creative, strategic and visionary, and as such will be less focused on the more disciplined operational side of the organisation. That's why leadership has to include a strong operational dimension.

Growth is great but it brings problems with it. You are growing like *nobody's business*, shooting for the stars, promising the world everything, but back at the ranch the operations and administration function is screaming. Why are they screaming? They are screaming because the organisational systems and processes are not sufficiently developed and resourced in order to consistently deliver the promise to the substantial, and growing, customer base. As a result, orders are missed, mistakes are made, paperwork is all over the place and people are getting hacked off. Blame culture kicks in, people aren't happy, and things are just not running well anymore. Sack the guilty? Well possibly, but what is the source of your problem? It can perhaps be fixed by using better organisational structures, systems and processes. *Get good systems and processes in place and the problems may not happen* is the thinking at this stage.

For leadership – the next move is that they need to put in more structures, systems and processes to kill off the tension. Leadership now needs to include not just entrepreneurial and operational types but also a strong administrator type leader to bring order, good administration and financial systems into the organisation. For example, this could be in the form of a financial director, or an administration manager. So, more structures, systems and processes are added, some new staff members are employed and things are starting to be more effectively and efficiently led throughout the organisation. Creativity and innovation is still encouraged by entrepreneurial leaders, but the more operational or administrative types of leaders are making sure that systems and processes are given equal attention so that the organisation continues to grow efficiently, and consistently deliver for the customer.

HOWEVER, WHEN YOU GROW, YOU HAVE TO GROW UP, IN TERMS OF BUILDING IN GOOD ORGANISATIONAL STRUCTURES, SYSTEMS AND PROCESSES TO ENSURE EVERYTHING OPERATES EFFICIENTLY AND EFFECTIVELY.

LEADING TO STAY UP!

Staying up and remaining innovative, profitable and competitive is possible but it requires keeping the right balance between a creative and innovative culture which adapts to change and stays relevant to the market, and good systems to make it all work efficiently and effectively. So far, you have got out of the danger zone of the start-up phase and justified your existence by proving that people actually want the stuff that you sell and you can do it profitably. You have built momentum and started to move on the *way up* and grow in terms of new customers but you are also growing organisationally, putting good systems and processes in place and ensuring you continue to achieve your goals. As a leader you have also worked your way through the challenges of operations, administration and sales functions, who have been at each other's throats because nothing seems to work anymore, because sales have shot ahead of the development of the organisational capacity to deliver the promises. New systems, structures and staff have been introduced, stuff that works is kept and stuff that doesn't (including people) have been dumped. The whole thing is now looking *pretty mint!*

At this stage in the game, the organisation has an innovative and creative environment, with a high level of profitability and a high level of entrepreneurial activity and employee engagement. The key issue is staying at the top! Staying on top is "good", not staying at the top is "bad". Leadership needs to sustain this position. And to do that, essentially it is about balance in the environment that has been created. And that is to create a balance of entrepreneurial zeal, creativity and risk taking, with the right level of organisational systems and processes. Leadership needs to make sure that the culture of creativity and innovation, that propelled the organisation forward to double digit growth, continues to be sustained.

LEADING "ON THE WAY DOWN"

The problem is that keeping the right balance is not always that easy, and if an organisation is around long enough the balance can be tipped in the wrong direction. For various reasons, an organisation can just lose its edge, and become less innovative. When any environment that is created grows in size, there are more people, things are more complex, more problems, more issues and all this can crowd out the culture of creativity and innovation. At the start of the journey you have simplicity, and as you progress on through that journey everything just gets more complex. Three people worked fine together in the early days but three hundred people is a different matter altogether. And the only way it can work is for leadership to apply new and effective structures, systems and processes. However, over time structures, systems and processes can grow in complexity too. One word – bureaucracy! And in a bureaucracy things tend to rapidly become boring! The place is more like a machine rather than a movement. There is still a lot of sales activity, and market share: the buzz is still there. However, there is an underlying cultural shift from creativity, innovation and risk taking, to a more managerial, bureaucratic environment that actually starts to discourage risk taking and innovation.

Due to the fact that things are starting to be inward looking rather than outward looking, at this stage the customer is, strangely, starting to get a bit, well, annoying! That customer, whom the organisation used to love to bits, has started to become a bit of a hassle, a nuisance, and maybe not so loved at this stage! Leadership essentially needs to "get it" at this stage. The leaders need to "get it" that things have moved in the wrong direction. It's too formalised and it's too rigid and overly complex. The entrepreneurial, innovative and creative people are starting to leave the building because it is becoming bureaucratic. And the organisation is starting to attract a disproportionate number of bureaucratic, risk averse individuals! So it is very simple, the leaders across the organisation now need to just "get it." They need to see that the environment is moving the wrong way and needs to be pulled back from the brink.

If you don't "get it" then it's tail spin time! You are on the way down rapidly. That unique culture which propelled the organisation to growth and success with its relevant offering to the world, has started to become increasingly irrelevant due to its failure to innovate, adapt to change and see to it that its offering to the market is still right for their customer. Entrepreneurial zeal, innovation and flexibility in an organisation are getting lost and anyone in the organisation that is characterised in this way has either left or is leaving! The organisation is determined to keep efficient, profitable and compliant with the systems and processes that have been created, and devotes all its energy to this.

The customer is no longer the centre of attention, and instead focus is on internal needs. And because of all this obsessive navel gazing, the customer is now really annoying and it (the customer is now an "it" at this stage!) can now put up or shut up! If the customer doesn't like it – tough! If the customer leaves – then good riddance. And because the organisation no longer loves the customer, it doesn't care, and because it doesn't care the organisation doesn't ask how the customer is feeling and what he or she needs and wants! Therefore at this stage the customer isn't being listened to. And human nature being what it is, in any relationship, if we don't feel listened to, special and cared for – we move on! Customers are no different – they move on! At this stage, the organisation is in so much trouble it is not even funny. The stuff that they are firing out into the market place is just junk! There has been no innovation and therefore no new competitive offering that meets the requirements of the changing customer habits and needs.

Quite simply, the organisation is just no longer relevant. People are leaving the burning building, and customers are leading the charge and going to competitors who are on the way up or staying up on their journey. The organisation is on its way out! It is over! And do you know what? No one cares less! Why? People are only concerned if you are relevant and because you haven't been relevant to them then no one cares that the organisation is in its final death pangs. Sure we will all shed the crocodile tears displayed for those long established businesses that we bought our sweets from when we were young and indulge in a little nostalgia - but that is it. When the company folds, the next day the customer will have moved on in every sense of the word.

Leadership, if they have been the cause of this, should be looking to move on too - because the organisation will soon no longer exist!

Obviously, no leader wants to be in this situation. As Chris Tarrant from the TV show, *Who wants to be a Millionaire?* used to say: "But... we don't want to give you that!" So leaders don't want that, leaders want to stay on top. How do they do it? How do they structure the organisation in a way that avoids heading face down in the doggy doo?!

STAYING AT THE TOP – HAVE A VISION OF BEING RELEVANT

Leadership needs to have a fresh look at why the organisation exists. Is it still relevant? Does it still solve a problem in the market that many are suffering from, and do those people want a solution, and are you able to offer that solution at a price less than the cost of enduring that problem? If you can say "Yes" to this then you are relevant. Then you have to ask – "Are we as relevant as our competitors or are we as relevant as we should be?" It is likely that you are not hitting the spot as you should. So you are now on a journey to be highly relevant, more relevant than anyone in your market. You need to set out your vision for achieving this goal, and then your strategy for how you are going to get there, through having a dynamic organisation that delivers creativity and innovation with a good balance of effective world class structures, systems and processes.

STAYING AT THE TOP - STRIKING THE RIGHT BALANCE

Striking the right balance of leadership roles (entrepreneurial, operational, and administrative) is what is important. As an example of all these roles working together, let me go back to my brief spell as a rather poor photocopier sales rep. Back then if I did actually manage to sell one of those machines, I typically went to the client when the photocopier was being delivered to them. Mostly to avoid the pain of trying to sell more of the blinking things, but also to witness that the customer had actually followed through and bought the photocopier! Anyway the decision as to where the photocopier *should be located* - from a leadership perspective - goes something like this:

The operational leader will just want to get the photocopier put into the office, will want to move it straight away, and will probably not ask anyone's opinion and not consider the implications too deeply.

The administrative leader will think about health and safety implications and if the new location will be efficient for the staff. And he/she probably will still be querying whether we could have got it at a cheaper price!

LEADERSHIP NEEDS TO HAVE A FRESH LOOK AT WHY THE ORGANISATION EXISTS. IS IT STILL RELEVANT? DOES IT STILL SOLVE A PROBLEM IN THE MARKET THAT MANY ARE SUFFERING FROM, AND DO THOSE PEOPLE WANT A SOLUTION, AND ARE YOU ABLE TO OFFER THAT SOLUTION AT A PRICE LESS THAN THE COST OF ENDURING THAT PROBLEM?

The entrepreneurial leader will think nothing because they will not even have known (or much care) that the photocopier will have been purchased, but when he/she does see it he/she probably will ask the question: *Could we get some reciprocal business from the photocopier supplier?* And then spend the rest of the day playing with the photocopier like a kid with a big toy on Christmas day!

All of these leadership roles are important for any organisation. The entrepreneurial role keeps things moving forward through innovation, risk taking and a relentless focus on growing a competitive and successful organisation. The operational type leader will make sure that everything is running like clockwork back at the ranch, to ensure that operationally the organisation delivers over and over again for the customer. And the administrator type leader makes sure that the right balance of systems and processes are in place to maintain efficiency but sustain creativity and innovation within the culture.

Obviously, these leadership types can clash! The classic clash of leaders will be between the entrepreneurial leader and the administrator type leader. They will butt heads because, yes, they are both leaders focusing on creating an environment to achieve goals, but their focus will be different and sometimes appear contradictory. In other words, the entrepreneurial leader will be focused on entering a new market to grow the company, and pay little attention (or interest) to the administrative changes that need to be made in order to service that new market (changes in invoices, tax differences, legal compliance etc). To the entrepreneurial leader – all that administrative stuff is "boring!" However, to the administrator type leader it is necessary and of equal importance to get the right systems in place. Both want to grow, both want to enter the new market, but both have different priorities. I remember the first time I (entrepreneurial type leader) won a big consultancy contract of £150,000, and I rang my financial manager (administrator type leader) to tell her the great news. *"We won, we won, we won!"* I said excitedly. However, she calmly replied, *"What is the budget, what is the profitability and how do we claim for our money?"* *"I don't care...* *"We won, we won, we won!"* as I ran around the office in excitement and punched the air! See the difference.

There is a solution to these types of clashes. We can take a whole section here on the interventions. However, I am an entrepreneurial leader not an HR expert so my simple solution, is *Dry your eyes, see where everyone is coming from, talk it out and get on with it!*

STAYING AT THE TOP - LEADERSHIP STRUCTURE...
GREY DOESN'T WORK!

At the final interview stage, my future Managing Director said to me, "You know Phil, the management structure in this organisation is a bit grey... can you work with that?" I promptly replied, "Yeah, I can work with that." Fast forward six months, and my answer would have been: "No, I can't work with that!" Keep structures simple in a way that doesn't cause confusion to leadership or staff. Grey, ambiguous structures cause all sorts of problems. And where there is grey and ambiguity then people exploit it. For example, if a general manager has a responsibility for sales, but the operational remit is in the hands of the operations manager then without a doubt the operational staff who are notionally under the general manager will exploit this!

Confused? Well that's what happens with "grey structures". Keep things black and white, with clear lines of reporting. Let there be leaders with autonomy and authority and head space to achieve the goals that they have been tasked with.

STAYING AT THE TOP – REVIEW WHO DOES WHAT (IN REALITY)

As time goes on through the organisational journey, sometimes people's job title and role do not reflect the reality of what they are actually doing on a daily basis. Who they are supposed to be reporting to may not be the actual person they are reporting to and so on. It is important to have a fresh look at the organisational chart every so often to examine whether it reflects the reality on the ground. It can also reveal whether someone has too many people reporting into them or not enough!

A good realistic organisational chart can highlight visually how the business functions in reality and the areas that need to be addressed to see that it remains effective and efficient in achieving its goals. Make sure you try and break down walls.

Try to get simple, straightforward structures that work and make sense and allow for the flexibility and adaptability that enable the organisation to stay fresh and innovative.

STAYING AT THE TOP – GET LEADERS TO WORK TOGETHER...

Leaders more often than not will lead with other leaders. Each leader has got their task of creating an environment that enables goals to be achieved. The Financial Director is busy creating an environment to ensure their financial team knock out the right numbers; similarly the Sales Director is doing the same to ensure their sales reps hit their targets and so forth. The mark of great leaders is their ability to work laterally.

Some leaders will just report up the chain of command and not work together with their peer leaders. It must be explained to everyone that they must work laterally with others and this is now a fundamental principle in the organisation. **Rather than only meeting when there is an issue or a crisis, leaders need to meet with each other regularly to discuss improvements, opportunities, and to brainstorm.**

STAYING AT THE TOP – GET EVERYONE TO WORK TOGETHER

One of the greatest tensions in a business in my experience is between operations and commercial. Fundamentally, I believe the tension comes down to a problem of communication which is at the heart of a breakdown in any relationship. For example, the commercial function signs a contract to deliver 1000 widgets in blue on Tuesday, but at the last minute before delivery the client changes the order to the colour red. The commercial function agrees to do the magic and commits to delivering the changed order on the same day, with operations left to work around the clock to deliver the promise made by the sales guy. The commercial function can over commit; they can promise service offerings that are unrealistic at worst or can cause significant strain on operational resources at best. It is essential that these two functions are regularly meeting and talking together in your organisation. Form cross functional teams of commercial and operations staff that work together on various projects, improve efficiencies, new service offerings and even sales strategies. By doing this, then it will bring greater coherence, eliminate problems, reduce tension and bring greater harmony.

STAYING AT THE TOP – CHALLENGE AND ACCOUNTABILITY FOR EVERYONE!

Human nature is what it is – flawed, very flawed. And we all need boundaries and parameters in our world in order to keep us focused, effective, and to avoid drift. At every stage in the organisational journey there should be a strong accountability and challenge function. Everyone needs to be held accountable for the role that they have and they are tasked with fulfilling. It is every leader's responsibility to ensure that whatever environment he or she is leading, that environment must have accountability and challenge throughout the organisation.

HOLDING PEOPLE TO ACCOUNT:

First of all your staff need to know what they are being held accountable for! Have they formally been given the expectations of their role, its requirements, anticipated outputs, and targets? Do they know what you expect of them? Make sure you have that conversation formally. Then revisit that discussion every six months (or whatever frequency you think necessary) in order that there be no confusion or misunderstanding. The people

HUMAN NATURE IS WHAT IT IS — FLAWED, VERY FLAWED. AND WE ALL NEED BOUNDARIES AND PARAMETERS IN OUR WORLD IN ORDER TO KEEP US FOCUSED, EFFECTIVE, AND TO AVOID DRIFT. AT EVERY STAGE IN THE ORGANISATIONAL JOURNEY THERE SHOULD BE A STRONG ACCOUNTABILITY AND CHALLENGE FUNCTION.

you lead should know, and you yourself should definitely know, what they need to be delivering.

Secondly, there should be a clear understanding of implications of delivering or under delivering. The people you lead should understand very clearly what happens, both positive or negative, if they exceed expectations or under perform. That should be clear and there should be no misunderstanding. In a company I used to work for there was a target for the sales reps that had to be achieved within three weeks of starting their job. They knew what it was, they were given the tools to achieve it, but failure to achieve those sales results led to instant dismissal. It may seem harsh but everyone knew what was expected (realistic or otherwise) and they knew the consequences if it wasn't achieved. No surprises and no awkward conversations.

CHALLENGING YOUR PEOPLE

People need to be held accountable but also challenged to continue to develop and grow. Everyone needs to be challenged about their performance, challenged to train more, learn more, and be more creative or whatever you feel they need to focus on in order to better achieve the goals.

Challenging should be peppered with encouragement and support, affirmation and confirmation of their strengths and successes. And whatever you are challenging them on, it has to be directly linked to the overall goals of the organisation.

You may challenge them about their aloof personality or weird dress sense (probably better not doing this!) but neither may be relevant to their ability to achieve goals for the organisation.

Challenge on areas that are relevant and that are necessary, making clear that it is for their betterment and the betterment of the organisation as a whole. Make sure they know and understand that - and it is not challenging for challenging's sake.

STAYING AT THE TOP – HAVE A DESTROY AND DELEGATE MANTRA

The organisation has to ensure that irrelevant processes, paper, (and people) are taken out of the equation.

Everyone needs to be on a journey of simplicity of process and ensure that documents that are not needed are destroyed, inefficient or unnecessary processes are eliminated, and underperforming or unproductive people are taken out of the environment (i.e. *sacked*... lest there be any confusion or misunderstanding!). With a strong accountability function, people will shoulder personal responsibility for the processes they adopt and for justifying whether it is relevant and being done in the best way.

Delegation needs to be flowing within the organisation, and leaders, managers and co-ordinators need to master this art, so that their staff are empowered to make decisions and to increase their sphere of responsibility and skills sets. This also frees up time for managers to start to think and act like leaders and become more strategic, and more focused on taking things to the next level.

STAYING AT THE TOP - CONFRONT THE BRUTAL FACTS

When times are good (can you remember those days?!) and profits are being made and all is well in the world there are many underlying issues and problems in our businesses that we simply don't deal with. We don't deal with them because... well we don't need to! Or we think we don't need to! The underperforming sales rep isn't removed, the inefficient process is tolerated and the unprofitable product line is ignored because to confront these problems can be too painful. The business does well despite these problems and, to use that terrible line, "We just kick the can down the road," to be dealt with another day, or not, if we can avoid it. My Managing Director used to always ring me before a Board meeting and say, "What good news do we have for the board?" There was a stack of bad news that needed to be dealt with, weakness that needed to be addressed, threats that had to be countered, but he didn't want to know and he assumed, I think wrongly, the board didn't want to know either.

In my view, good news will take care of itself, it's the bad stuff that won't and it is the bad stuff that can ultimately destroy a company. During times of plenty we can feel that we have the luxury of being able to ignore these internal business weaknesses because we think, "Hey we are making money, so why rock the boat!" However, when times are tough and the business is facing difficult challenges we must confront brutal facts about the underlying weaknesses within our business.

Dealing with problems, making painful changes, dumping unprofitable contracts and having difficult conversations with staff are not things I relish and I suspect I am not the only one. If you are the type of manager/leader who comfortably confronts long-standing issues and problems in an organisation, then save yourself some time and flip to the next section... you have mastered something many have not. If you are like me, however, keep reading.

The starting point in overcoming the challenges of growing your business during a recession is to confront some brutal facts about you and your organisation. To do that we have to ask ourselves four very simple questions:

1. **What is the business good at and how can we repeat it?**

    Over the last twelve months, what area has the business performed well in? It could be that your business is great at securing new contracts or that you are managing your cash flow well. Whatever it is you are good at write it down and then focus on how you are going to repeat it. The key thing is embedding that "good thing you do" in the organisation to make sure that it is not dependent on an individual or group of individuals who may one day leave the organisation.

2. What is the business bad at and how can we stop it?

Over the last twelve months, what has your business performed badly in? It could be that your business is bad at credit control or your customer service has become inconsistent. Whatever it is you are bad at write it down and focus on how you are going to sort the problem out. The key thing is to address "why" it is happening and to look at the root cause of the problem rather than just tackle the more obvious "what" is going wrong.

3. What product, process or person is preventing success and what are we going to do about that?

This may be obvious or it may require some searching. One thing is guaranteed, if you are not growing or you want to grow more, then you have to address anything that is preventing your business moving forward. We avoid confronting these weaknesses for understandable reasons. We can be emotionally attached to a process that is inefficient because we ourselves created it, or we can ignore an unprofitable product line because our customers like it, and we can keep hold of the wrong person because they have been there from the start and have always been loyal. Yes... our inertia is understandable but we have to move on it.

4. **What product, process or person is driving success and what are we going to do about that?**

This again may be obvious or it may require some searching. There are key players, profitable product lines and slick processes that all "just work". What is the reason for their success, why are they working so well and how can we make the whole organisation just as good? Beyond that, how do we make sure all those good people stay and keep performing, those processes keep efficient and that product remains profitable? All these issues have to be addressed.

These questions are designed to confront the brutal facts about your business. They have to be answered honestly and the issues have to be addressed with urgency. There may be an argument, perhaps a weak argument, for adopting a "head in sand" mentality during the boom periods, but when we want to grow our business during challenging economic conditions we must deal with the internal weaknesses in our business. Let's face it... we can't do anything about the external factors impacting on our organisation so we might as well focus on the things that we can change!

FRESH EYES

Sometimes it can be useful to bring someone in from the outside (a business adviser or just a trusted business colleague) to have a look at how you do things and give you a fresh, detached non-emotive perspective on how the organisation functions and whether the structures, systems and processes are effective and efficient for the goals that are set.

INFRASTRUCTURE + PEOPLE + ORGANISATION = CULTURE

Having made sure the infrastructure bit is right, the people bit is right and the organisation bit is also right – all of that will lead to a culture. A culture can be great or it can be woeful. A great leader has to make it great. And great means that it is a culture that adapts to change and ensures that the organisation stays relevant for employees, customers, the market and anyone who cares! Oh, and importantly, that it is a culture that everyone loves. How do you create this culture? Read on.

LEADERSHIP
AND CULTURE

CREATE A CULTURE THAT PEOPLE LOVE

You must have a desire to create a culture that people love. That's where it begins – with a desire and a determination of the will. Nothing great happens unless you desire it and determine that it will happen. If you don't care about creating this culture it will never happen. If you only do it because it is something you read in a text book (or this book) – then forget it. Do it because it is the right thing to do. Determine that you will create an environment that people will just love to bits and never want to leave.

You must then discipline yourself and others to now create that culture that everyone will love. And let's face it, it's not that difficult! Just do the right things! Delegate and empower people to do great things. Encourage and help people on their journey. Provide opportunities for development and progression. Care for people, make sacrifices. And encourage and hold to account everyone to do the same.

LEADERS KEEP CALM... SET THE TONE

Leaders need to be calm, everyone needs to stay calm. A culture where everyone is nasty, losing their heads, arguing and freaking out at every situation is a disaster and a horrendous environment to work in. So leadership needs to set the tone and here is how to do it.

- **Act of the will**

  Determine that you will be calm. Obvious point but some people see "psyching out" as inevitable, understandable and perhaps even necessary. It's none of these things - determine to keep calm and lead!

LEADERS NEED TO BE CALM,
EVERYONE NEEDS TO STAY
CALM. A CULTURE WHERE
EVERYONE IS NASTY, LOSING
THEIR HEADS, ARGUING AND
FREAKING OUT AT EVERY
SITUATION IS A DISASTER
AND A HORRENDOUS
ENVIRONMENT TO WORK IN.

- **Hold your tongue**

  My instinct is always to speak up, get into the debate, and start to give my opinions. Leaders need to discipline themselves at times to just say nothing. Listen to what is being said, observe, formulate your views based on data and facts rather than he said/she said nonsense, and only then consider opening your mouth. You are not only a voice of calm but someone conveying an intelligent narrative of *solution giving* and *situation sorting* leadership which people will respect.

- **Walking**

  My previous book *Start to Grow* mentions the benefits of walking. Sometimes you just need to get out of the pressured environment to clear the head, get your thoughts together and de-stress a bit. You should be calmer after a few miles' hike!

- **Communication**

  Great Leaders have to be master communicators. Use that gift. Have one-on-ones, seek advice, and listen to what people have to say. Understand the situation and where everyone is coming from. Get them to take emotion out of the environment and start to focus on sorting the issue.

- **Balanced approach**

  A leader must approach crisis situations in a balanced way. Too little action or reaction to a situation and the issue doesn't get resolved; too much action or reaction and it gets ugly. A leader is balanced, ensuring responses are dealt with, using exactly the right measure of involvement.

I remember many years ago, before starting up ShredBank, that I was in the middle of leading a business through a crisis and it was a major crisis. There was blood on the wall (not literally but there could have been). Through most of the time I kept my cool when many around me were doing the very opposite. However, at one point, when I thought no one was looking and in a moment of exasperation and exhaustion I put my face in my hands. And as I looked up a few seconds later, one of the staff members was standing with their jaw dropped looking at me in absolute shock and terror that I was now waving the white flag. In leadership, don't let them see you bleed. Well you can, but it isn't great leadership.

DEALING WITH OFFICE POLITICS - BREAKING THE CYCLE

Office politics is essentially about relationships. You can't and never will stop office politics. It is the stuff of life. Some people gel and others don't. Some people back bite and others tell it to your face. Some people are divisive, and others seek unity where they go. It is a microcosm of the outside world – a mixture of good, bad and ugly with different opinions, points of view and personalities. And the truth is always tricky to see. There are never two sides to every story - there is always a third side. The third side of the story is the truth.

DEALING WITH OFFICE POLITICS -

HAVE VALUES

Respect, honesty, and integrity are some of the ones to consider as values for your company. Make sure they are visible for all to see. And it is crucial that the leader lives and breathes them and sets the example. Hold people to account on them and consider integrating them into the performance appraisals.

DON'T LET ISSUES FESTER

Whether it is an issue between two colleagues, a person bent on causing disunity or an ongoing process failure, it is crucial that you deal with it there and then. "Kicking the can down the road" to be dealt with another day just never works. Deal with it, nip it in the bud, and sort out the issue real quick.

RECRUIT ON CHARACTER

Negative office politics can be eased if you have the right people. Recruit on character. You are looking for people who are strong on values and can give evidence of such. You are looking for people who believe in teamwork, respect, and give you a good answer on the "Office Politics Question"!

A CULTURE OF "EQUITY", "NEUTRALITY" AND "CONSISTENCY"

Here are three ways in which your leadership and culture should play out. There should be **equity, neutrality** and **consistency**. A leader should treat everyone with equity. In other words, everyone should be treated the same. Now, undoubtedly because everyone has different roles and different abilities and people are at different stages, you will inevitably spend time with some more than others. However, it is how you treat them that is key and that should always be done with equity. A leader should also be neutral, in that there should be no perception of bias when dealing with, for example, conflict or promotion. The leader should be above making decisions for emotive or likeability reasons. Regarding consistency, if you move on one under performer then you have to move on all of them! If you bonus one person then you have to bonus others for exceeding their targets. There has to be consistency. For a leader, the triple goal of equity, neutrality and consistency is painfully hard to achieve, costly, and can be a right headache – but great leaders must aim for it and persuade others to do the same.

A CULTURE OF CLEAR HEADS

I suggest that everyone needs to have a clear desk, clear inbox policy. Greatness is built on the basics and in order to do great things you have to sort the basics out. If you can't think straight you will never think creatively. If your desk is full of files and paper, your inbox has three hundred unread messages and everything is organisationally behind and all over the place then you will not think creatively. Clear out the desks and inboxes, clear the decks and you will be able to think more creatively.

A CULTURE OF CREATIVITY AND INNOVATION

A culture of creativity and innovation that adapts to change and ensures your organisation remains relevant can be achieved by doing the following:

GIVE PEOPLE PERMISSION

People need to feel they have the freedom to **think and reflect.** Yes think and reflect. So often our daily tasks just involve doing what needs to be done. It can often be the case that we don't stop, or take time out to think and reflect on how we can improve things, make a process more efficient, and come up with new ideas to bring the organisation closer to its goals. Life can so often be about the tactical rather than the strategic. And in an organisation the culture can be dominated by tactical rather than strategic thinking. I don't want to be too prescriptive here but give your people time to breathe, think, and reflect.

They also need permission to **collaborate.** Allow people, teams, departments and divisions to come together and collaborate together formally and informally, ad hoc and more permanently to improve co-ordination, team building and cohesiveness.

People need to feel also that they can **disagree** with you and others, but particularly you. There is nothing worse than a spirit of fear leading to a culture of head nodders who are terrified of turning around to their line manager and saying, "I don't agree with that approach, there is a better way." It is not easy to do but every so often when you ask someone to do something, ask them, "Do you agree?" or "Now be honest - do you think there is a better solution?"

People need to have permission to **invent,** to come up with new ideas, new products, new processes, new programmes, new projects or whatever new stuff your organisation could profit from. Again, the outworking of this will be up to each individual leader but people need to be given some time and some space to come up with new things as long as they are bringing the organisation closer to its goals.

And finally, people need permission to be **different!** A culture of diversity and different opinions is fresh and ensures creativity and innovation and, led right, healthy tensions that can spur the organisation on to achieve great and wonderful things beyond even its stated goals. Be different and stay creative.

LIFT UP YOUR HEAD AND LOOK AROUND

Again, it is easy to get into a bit of a rut in any organisation where we all get caught up in the internal issues. Focusing on running the organisation with a bit of crisis management here, and a bit of office politics there! However, to maintain and develop a culture of creativity we need to lift our heads and look around at the big bad world outside.

My business partner and I would either together or individually make a habit of going to industry trade shows. We would head off to the States or to Europe just to get out of the office, see new developments in the industry, speak to suppliers and other shredding business heads, just to get the creative juices flowing. Meeting new people, having conversations and listening to what is going on, is all part of keeping yourself and your organisation fresh. I personally would also go to business conferences and events completely unrelated to the shredding industry to see what other industries are doing and to see what is happening generally in the economy and in the world. This is all very important for keeping that culture of creativity. And don't just lift your head up and look around, provide opportunities for other people across your organisation to do the same.

GET MENTORING

Many people don't take risks, innovate or be creative because they are just plain scared. They could do it, but they won't because they are afraid of lifting their head above the parapet and getting it whacked off by their boss. So people stay quiet, they don't suggest any new ideas, they don't speak when they see something being done that is inefficient, and they generally keep their mouth shut to avoid any consequences to them. Therefore, to avoid this rather stifling culture developing it is important to introduce mentoring into the organisation in order that people can make changes, innovate and be creative without fear.

The mentor should encourage his mentees to develop personally, to introduce improvements in his/her own environment and the company's environment and make sure they are kept in line with overall organisational goals. With a mentor, this can be done without fear of consequence, fear of getting it in the neck and fear of getting sacked! Making mistakes without fear, taking chances without fear and experimenting without fear are all part of creating that desired culture of creativity and innovation.

GET THE RIGHT PEOPLE IN!

Poor hiring will increase the problem of a lack of creativity and innovation. If you continuously bring in head nodding, tactical thinking, compliant people then it's going to make the problem systemic. You need to make sure that you bring in those who can prove at interview process that they are people who do think, reflect and collaborate and who do aim for a "zero inbox" mentality and can give examples of creativity and innovation throughout their education, and career. In order to achieve this, you need to hire competitively. In other words, you need to hire both internally and externally. You also need to make sure that when interviewing people you should ask them to give you examples of when they had to introduce something new into the organisation in order to achieve organisational goals. They should tell you what they did, why they did it, how they went about it, and what were the tangible impacts and outcomes of their act of creativity and innovation.

PUT IT IN THE PERFORMANCE APPRAISAL

If you have performance appraisals, then make sure that you encourage creativity and innovative activity in every role in the organisation. The performance appraisals should be addressing both successes and failures in this area. Areas to be assessed with employee should be the use of creativity and innovation, what they did differently, and improvements that they made. The employee should feel relaxed about making suggestions about areas for improvement within the organisation. What is working, what can be improved, and how things can be done better should be the nature of the discussions by both parties. The employee should then have an action plan to improve performance in the period ahead which he/she will be held accountable for but also potentially rewarded if implemented successfully. By implementing this, then the performance assessment process will strengthen the organisation's culture of creativity and innovation.

TRAINING AND DEVELOPMENT

Provide training that encourages innovation and creativity. The training has to ensure that people are developing their skills and abilities that go beyond just compliance with the existing systems and processes within the organisation. Ongoing, continuous training around innovation and creativity throughout the organisation is vital in order to ensure that there is a vibrant culture of change, adaptability, flexibility, new ideas, creativity and innovation!

SUSTAINING A CULTURE OF CREATIVITY AND INNOVATION

Leaders need to ensure that there is a healthy culture of risk taking but it must have parameters set around the overall goals of the organisation to avoid the scenario where a lot of crazy stuff is happening with very little relevance to the goals of the organisation. That risk taking culture also needs to have appropriate oversight through good mentoring relationships flowing throughout the organisation.

Sustaining a culture of creativity and innovation is about striving for a balance between maintaining the systems and processes needed to keep the organisation efficient and effective, and avoiding those systems and processes becoming so complex that they stifle innovation and creativity.

CREATIVITY AND
INNOVATION MUST BE
FLOWING THROUGHOUT
THE WHOLE ORGANISATION
RATHER THAN RESTING ON
JUST ONE INDIVIDUAL.

Leadership must keep that balance if they are to remain relevant in the long term in a rapidly changing world. In order to maintain that balance, creativity and innovation must be flowing throughout the whole organisation rather than resting on just one individual. This is for obvious reasons, because if the source of innovation and risk taking rests with one individual or group of individuals, then if those innovative individuals go – then the innovation and risk taking in the organisation also goes! So that's why everyone needs to be trained and encouraged to think creatively, everyone needs to be encouraged and challenged to be innovative and creative through performance appraisals and mentoring, and everyone needs to be given that space and room to think differently and make changes that will enable goals to be achieved.

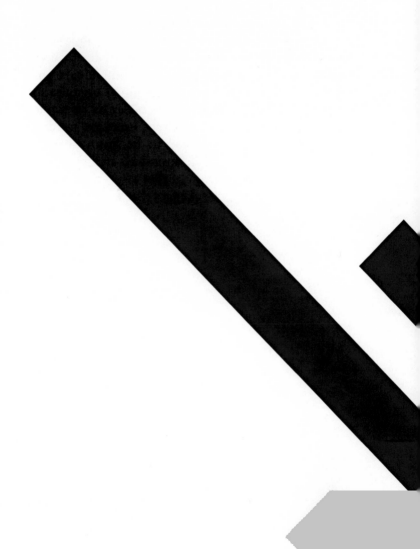

LEADERSHIP IN DIFFERENT CONTEXTS

A VOLUNTARY ORGANISATION

I have been on countless boards in the voluntary sector on both sides: as an employee reporting to the board, and as a Chair or board member holding people's feet to the fire. With my involvement in these, I learned a number of key lessons about a voluntary board:

- **Be realistic about your goals... you are just voluntary**

    When everyone comes together in a voluntary capacity for a board meeting, there can be a tendency to treat the meeting as if everyone around the table is employed on a permanent basis. Commitments are made and goals are set which can be great and very exciting, but you have to remember that everyone around the table is doing this for "FREE!" They are doing it on a voluntary basis, their time allocation for voluntary work is consciously or subconsciously limited. So be realistic when setting your activities, goals and targets for the voluntary directors around the table, as they can only do so much!

- **Third/ third/ third rule**

    In all my years of experience with any board, committee or for that matter any group of people coming together to achieve a goal, the third-third-third rule applies. And this is how it goes. One third does practically everything, another third does a bit of work but they need to be pulled along, and the final third does nothing. If you have been involved with any group at all trying to achieve a goal then you will know that the third-third-third rule always applies. And here's the thing - if you are part of the "Do nothing third" get out of the seat and resign. Create a space for someone who actually cares and will fulfil the role!

- **Create "Champions"**

  Don't just have random directors with no titles or responsibilities. Give each board member a specific responsibility so they can "Champion" that particular area. For example, you can have a director who is a sales and marketing expert being the Champion for marketing and PR, or a solicitor can be a Champion for legal issues, or a sales executive who could be Champion for fund raising. Review the type of specialist skills, knowledge and abilities your board needs and then recruit directors to match those requirements giving them responsibility for a particular area that they personally specialise in.

- **Get commitment**

  Make sure that there is a proper job description for each champion role on the board. Include the key skills, abilities, and experience required and also detail the job role and expectations. Include the approximate time commitment required from them, the number of board meetings, activities to attend, and the outputs of the role. Again, be realistic about what you are asking and expecting of a voluntary position, but get them to sign off on it and include also a formal one-to-one review process every six months so that you can evaluate their progress, commitment, ability and time to fulfil the role that they have committed to.

A SOCIAL ENTERPRISE

A social enterprise is essentially an organisation that exists to deliver social goals. And those goals are delivered by operating as a trading enterprise that generates profit, but with the profits being used for the overall social goals of the organisation. Essentially, social enterprises are profit making but not profit taking. There are no shareholders to profit from the enterprise and if the enterprise was ever sold as an entity then the money generated would not go to any individual or investor. Rather it would be distributed to address the social purposes of that organisation.

In my early career I worked for two social enterprises over a four year period. Both of these social enterprises specialised in advising other social enterprises through providing business consultancy and training. As general manager of these social enterprises, there were a number of lessons that I learned from the experience.

- **Enterprise first... and then the social bit**

  Social enterprises tend to attract individuals who have a heart for their community or a particular social cause. That is good and inevitable. However, if the focus is primarily directed towards the social goals of the social enterprise then the business side will not get enough attention, the organisation will not make any money and it will go under. Resulting in ultimately none of the social goals being achieved because the organisation doesn't exist! Social enterprises must operate like any other business in that they must get the business model right, they must focus on creating a sustainable enterprise that generates profit, and is self sustaining so that they can then deliver on their social goals.

- **The social enterprise board must have champions**

  Following on from what was said previously about voluntary boards, each board member must be champion of a specific area. Given that it is essentially a business that is operating - do not pack the board with the *great and the good* type of individuals who do the voluntary board circuit, packing their CV with a string of different voluntary positions. Make sure you put enterprise oriented individuals on the board, including entrepreneurs, business owners, accountants, social entrepreneurs, solicitors, marketers etc. Of course, it is important to populate the board with those perhaps non-commercial individuals who have particular expertise and experience that can help social goals to be achieved or ensure good corporate governance.

- **Show equity with the private sector**

  Sometimes in social enterprises there is a mindset that suggests that staff take a lower salary than their private sector peers because it is a social enterprise with social goals and therefore everyone should make the sacrifice for the greater good. Personally, I think this mindset is rubbish. Social enterprises need to build their organisations up as successful trading entities that can pay the same as private sector firms. In order to create a sustainable profitable and successful company that delivers over and above the social goals that have been set out, you need to attract exceptional people. And they don't come out of a Christmas cracker!

A FAITH BASED ORGANISATION

I am currently an Elder in Moira Baptist Church, and my late father was also an Elder of another church many years ago. I have seen leadership in church life from all angles and understand the joys and challenges that come with the role. Let me get straight to the stuff you need to understand about leading any faith based organisation:

- Spiritual purpose

  Why does the faith based organisation exist? You must spell that out and lay it out for everyone. Set out the purpose for the organisation's existence and determine that everything that is done should ultimately be about that purpose. The vision for our Church is to "Glorify God, Reflect Christ and Love People." Therefore, everything we do in our church essentially has to be about that. The church doesn't exist for me and my family, or for me to get something out of it. It is for a greater spiritual purpose.

- **Get the balance right**

  I believe that when it comes to faith and worship there is a balance that the church and its leaders have to be careful to support, encourage and enable. That balance is between the individual's worship, family worship and church worship. If there is too much time spent on an individual's spiritual journey then family and church get neglected. If too much focus is on church activities and church life then the family get no attention and neither do you! The balance must be right and leadership in faith based organisations needs to encourage that balance.

- **It's not a community centre**

  Let a community centre be a community centre and let a church be a church. Each has their own remit. A faith based organisation should focus on the spiritual. A community organisation can focus on the social, sports, and other activities. If you want sports and activities then go to a community or leisure centre. If you want focus on the spiritual then go to a church. Don't blur the lines. Leaders need to stick to the spiritual purpose, otherwise it will get lost and you will wake up some day to realise that you are leading a community centre rather than a faith based organisation.

- **Keep it simple**

  Like every organisation on the life cycle, it can grow and become more complex. Faith based organisations are no different. Churches can become swamped with committees, meetings, activities and programmes, and eventually people can burn out, get weary and lose focus on the spiritual purpose - which it is ultimately all about. Let the main thing be the main thing. As a leader, keep meetings to a minimum, keep structures simple, and keep everyone focused ensuring they have a healthy balance of individual, church and family focus in their lives.

A START-UP

Leadership in a start-up will largely be in the hands of the founder or owner. To lead a start-up is to lead entrepreneurially. You are creating and building an environment on a very time bound struggle (usually twelve months) to rebalance cash from internal sources (loans, investment, overdraft and personal money) with external cash (payment from customers). You will be likely leading a little team, with very little money and with few customers, but you will have big hopes, dreams and aspirations of taking on the world. Leading a start-up is getting out there and evangelising the world about the good news of what your business has to offer and inspiring and motivating your little team for true greatness! At this stage the leader's primary concern is selling and cash. That is it – selling and cash! Everything is about securing customers to justify the organisation's existence and to generate enough money from new customers to end the flow of internal funding (loans, investment, borrowings), and become self sustaining. It is a race against time because funding from internal sources no matter how much you have, will eventually dry up. So there is an urgency to establish a viable market before the initial cash runs out.

In terms of organisational systems and processes, there are very few of them because there are likely only a few people floating about and organisational charts are those things you read about in text books! Are there organisational policies, systems, procedures, and budget? No, not a one! There are none! Why? Because at this stage the leadership cares only about two things – get sales and cash! That's it and that's the priority. Oh, of course, we will talk the talk about putting in good systems and processes, but in my experience of leading six start-ups it is, and only ever will be at this stage about getting sales that will deliver the cash needed to survive. So at this point in the life cycle, the organisational structure is as flat as a pancake. Every man and his dog report to one person – the founder owner! That is the leader! Relationships at this stage are all personal; everyone knows each other and the few employees that may be about do everything that needs to be done with an intimate understanding of their customers – because there are only three of them!

So when it comes to leading a start-up here are some thoughts:

- **Sustainable profitable market**

  That is your mantra as a leader. You are there to find a "sustainable profitable market." You have established that your product or service solves a problem, and you have identified a number of people or organisations suffering that problem; you have a solution to their problem and you can provide it to them at a price less than the cost of enduring the problem in a way that delivers a customer experience that keeps them coming back for more and telling other people. And if you have that, then you must find this market, and make sure that you price and structure the solution appropriately, so that it is a profitable market that you can acquire, grow and become the leader in.

- **Brand awareness**

  If there is no brand awareness, then selling your products or services is nightmarishly difficult! The more brand awareness that there is for your products and services then the easier it will be in selling them to the market. Simple! Easy example is Coca-cola. It has huge brand awareness so I suspect selling Coke to the local restaurants and retailers is not that difficult! Through whatever means is relevant, right and legal, make sure you lead the charge in making your brand the go to, only option, forget all the others, I will pay the extra, brand that will enable you to create that long term sustainable profitable market that you need.

A FAST GROWTH BUSINESS

This is where you have connected with the market, you have got a number of customers under your belt and momentum has started to build with brand awareness growing, vigorous and relentless sales activity bearing much fruit, and customers being added more frequently. The turnover is growing, it's lifting every month and things are starting to really hum. The relationship between Operations function and Commercial function is pretty good at this stage as the Operations people are just delighted that business is coming in to justify their existence and sustain their jobs, and Commercial function love Operations because they are delivering consistently the promises that they have made to their new found customers. Sales is still the big focus and the picture is starting to emerge as to how much sales are needed to cover existing overheads and be profitable, but also what level of sales is needed to upscale and become a larger entity. Things are starting to become clear at this stage. What works and what doesn't work regarding sales, marketing, and the business model are all starting to become clearer.

In terms of systems and processes, it is all starting to fit into place. As the number of customers is starting to build up, systems are put in place to guarantee efficiency and effective delivery for the customer. IT systems are already being introduced, a good finance function is in place to make sure invoices, statements, payments, and credit control are all happening. Yes, the finance function may be a part-time person liaising with the owner and infrequently with the accountant but the point is that it is in place and it works well. At this stage, depending on the scale of the growth, there may be a functional manager or two being put in place as part of the leader needing to delegate. Leadership is still largely in the hands of the founders, but should now be encouraged within the organisation as a whole. So when it comes to leading a fast growth business here is one thought:

GROW UP!

The leadership role is to be now both entrepreneurial and organisational. The owner needs still to be in sales mode with that relentless drive to grab market share and be competitive, but the focus now has to be more balanced in that there is an organisational environment to create. There needs to be Administration, Operations, and Commercial functions put in place (albeit in some circumstances these functions will be at a very embryonic level). The leader will be developing those areas of infrastructure, culture, organisation, and people. Leadership should be encouraged across the organisation and those who have the management title should be encouraged, trained and developed to think and act like a leader.

A SMALL/MEDIUM ENTERPRISE

I suppose most of my business life has been in Small/Medium Enterprises and there is much that can be said in leading these types of businesses. However, here are a few things you need to watch for if you find yourself in leadership of an SME.

- **You are no longer a child**

  In leading an established SME you need to be careful that the organisation doesn't continue to operate and function as in the early days of its existence when the SME was, well, small. In those early beginnings, the structure of the business was simple, systems and processes were minimal and that was fine for the scale of the business and the number of customers it served. However, as the client base increases, and the organisation grows more complex, then it is important that the leader recognises this. The leader needs to develop the business *organisationally* in order to ensure efficiency and effectiveness, and a continuation of reliable delivery on its promises to its growing client base. New systems and processes need to be implemented, perhaps a review of some existing staff (so necessary in the early start-up, small business days but potentially redundant in the new era of the established SME), and you need to look at the organisational chart to see if it is still fit for purpose. The biblical verse of 1st Corinthians 13 comes to mind when thinking of the leadership transition from Start-up to established SME:

"When I was a child, I spoke as a child, I understood as a child, I thought as a child; but when I became a man, I put away childish things."

"THE LEADER NEEDS TO DEVELOP THE BUSINESS ORGANISATIONALLY IN ORDER TO ENSURE EFFICIENCY AND EFFECTIVENESS, AND A CONTINUATION OF RELIABLE DELIVERY ON ITS PROMISES TO ITS GROWING CLIENT BASE."

- **Management Accounts**

  I cover this in my *Start to Grow* book but I really am a bit of an evangelist for monthly management accounts delivered to your door by a good accountant. Part of the "putting away childish things" is to put away those practices that are common in the start-up days such as the *gung ho* attitude to financial management. Glancing at the bank balance and keeping a beady eye on the sales figures, whilst necessary and good at the time, is no longer the way to rigorously run the finances of your business and to ensure that you are solvent and profitable. Therefore, leadership of an SME is, among other things, about making sure that you have the complete financial picture of your organisation brought through good reliable management accounts.

- **Keeping it fun**

  "It just isn't fun anymore" will be the audible or inaudible cry of some of your staff who were around in the early start-up/growth days. Sometimes there can be acceptance in the organisation that the fun is over. However, it doesn't have to be over. It can't be the same type of crazy, wild fun of the early days, but you can still have a fun environment where the work still gets done and people are happy. Keeping it fun is not however about token staff dinners every six months! Keeping it fun means that people have clear direction and tasks to do that they will be held accountable for, but within those parameters they have got the head space to be themselves, to chat, to cultivate relationships, and to develop themselves through training etc. Keeping it fun means making sure the right people are in the organisation, doing the right job that fulfils them, and being given permission to be themselves and grow.

A LARGE ENTERPRISE/PUBLIC SECTOR

At board level and as a general manager, I have had the *fish out of water experience* of being involved in a number of large organisations. For me, in any large organisation you can guarantee two realities – things are complex and things are political. Complexity and politics are the order of the day and if you lead a large organisation this is essentially your brief – sort out the complexity and sort out the politics in order to ensure goals are achieved.

- **Politics**

  Politics is essentially about people and relationships. There will always be politics in any organisation regardless of size because where there are people, there are relationships, and where there are people and relationships there is politics. The issue in a large organisation is that the politics is more systemic and greater in its implications both strategically and operationally. If relationships break down at board level and the situation becomes highly toxic and divisive, then the organisation could well find itself facing the exit of a key executive and maybe the creation of a new competitor.

If there is a "them and us" culture developed between Commercial and Operations departments, then there will be commercial implications of the failure to collaborate and work cross-functionally - leading to poor service deliveries or overpromising and under-delivering for the customer. There can be under-performance by key personnel or key departments that for contractual and legal reasons may be very difficult to dislodge from the business despite the negative impact on the business. Or there may generally be, through the course of time, legacy issues of unresolved relationships problems, difficult people, and bruised egos of people overlooked in promotion that can make the political situation quite explosive.

As a leader, first of all don't beat yourself up about the fact that a large chunk of your time is being a politician in the midst of a political environment. Dealing with problematic relationships, managing out poor performers, accepting mediocrity within certain areas for the sake of political expediency, is all part of the political game that must be played.

As in all organisations consider the following when leading people:

1. Spheres of influence that one individual has on others

2. Alliances that you will need to be conscious of when making decisions

3. Political climate that needs to be managed

4. Power, and where it really lies

And like politics, it is a game and many are playing it. There will be those who are playing the game to get promotion, to get one over on someone or just simply to take their job. You have to be the political master in it all, understand it is a game, be relaxed that it is so, and play the game by being one step ahead of everyone else.

- **Complexity**

As organisations grow in scale to accommodate the delivery of the ever increasing size of the product/ service portfolio to the ever increasing number and diversity of customers, the organisation inevitably grows in complexity. The complexity is in the systems and processes that have to be embedded into the organisation to ensure that it continues to deliver the promise efficiently, effectively and profitably. Complexity sounds bad but it is actually good and necessary when an organisation hits a certain size. Complexity makes sure that there is a fully resourced finance department to chase payments, pay bills, and determine that the business stays solvent. Complexity will of necessity involve delegation, departments, managers, diversity of skills, and reporting mechanisms to ensure everything just works.

As a leader, again, be comfortable that you are leading complexity in a large organisation. It is inevitable. However, the leader at whatever level in a large organisation, must tame complexity to prevent it stifling the organisation's culture of innovation and risk taking which is necessary in adapting to change and remaining competitive and relevant to the world. Creating that culture of creativity and innovation is covered earlier in the book, but remember that the brief for any leader is not to destroy complexity but to make sure it is in the right balance. In other words, it's the Goldilocks scenario of "not too hot" and "not too cold" – things should be complex enough to ensure efficiency and retain creativity and innovation, but not so complex that there is a descent into an overly bureaucratic and inward looking organisation that will inevitably decline.

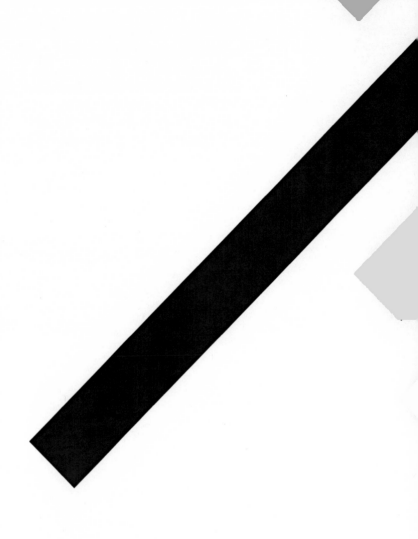

AND YOU...
HOW ARE
YOU DOING?

Yes, you. The reader! How are you doing? Anyone asked you that? Hopefully someone has but I wouldn't have been surprised if they haven't. Now, I don't mean someone casually saying "How's things?" With the anticipated "Not too bad" response or, "Yeah, things are good". I mean someone taking a genuine interest in YOU, looking YOU in the eye and asking a heartfelt, deeply concerned "How are you doing"?

Maybe you are doing fine but maybe you are feeling the very opposite of fine. Maybe you are feeling discouraged, weary, and perhaps fearful. Maybe you lack the passion you used to have, or maybe you are stressed and perhaps even depressed.

A leader looks in the mirror and they either grin or fade away. And if you haven't been grinning in a while then you are fading. What has happened? Probably you are weary, burnt out, done. The rollercoaster is grinding to a stop and you are sick as a dog with no interest whatsoever in jumping on another one! The thrill is gone.

If this is how you feel, there is no point sugar coating it – it isn't good. You are in the danger zone. That type of scenario can easily tip into unhealthy stress (as opposed to the healthy type which does actually exist) and even worse... depression. So what do you do when you find yourself fading away?

- **Take off**

  Take a long break. At least four weeks but it will probably need more. Disappear from everything. Switch the phones off, take yourself out of all your usual commitments and rest your mind and body.

- **Offload**

  Get rid of non-essential leadership stuff that you have got caught up in. Any committees, boards etc. - stand down from them either permanently or temporarily. You can have conversations with people just to let them know you are on temporary hiatus but you need to be at least relieved of duties for now. Or just outright quit everything!

- **Hydrate**

  Start drinking lots of water. All that stress will probably have dehydrated you - making your brain mush. Start drinking lots of water, every day. Pour the stuff into you.

- **Eat, exercise, sleep**

  Eat well and healthily, get lots of good sleep (go to bed at a reasonable hour and wake at a reasonable hour), and do thirty minutes of some exercise every day.

- **Change direction?**

  Consider if what you are now doing is what you want to be doing in the next few years. Perhaps this is the time for a complete change. Maybe you are just genuinely done with your current world and you need to move into another one. However, this is a radical step so you should first see if the taking off, offloading, drinking lots of water, eating well, sleeping and exercising has worked.

- **Refocus**

  Turn to that which really matters - family, friends and yourself. Life is about balance and perhaps you have just tipped it in the wrong direction. If you have, you need to refocus and pay attention to those great areas of your life that mean the most. However, as in everything as a leader, whatever you do – do the right things.

AND FINALLY

The world we live in is uncertain and there is chaos and confusion at every corner. Relationships are breaking down, people are never happy, and there is discontentment everywhere. And to top it off – nothing is getting sorted because of a culture of poor leadership. In light of this, the world is crying out for great leaders but the world is sadly left wanting in so many situations.

However, as you lift your head up after reading this book - start thinking of all the environments that you are involved in. Environments such as your family... your employment... perhaps a business... your relationships... maybe a voluntary or faith based organisation. And as you think of all the environments that you find yourself in - tell me one environment that does not need great leadership!? Those environments need someone to come in with a deep desire to see goals achieved and lives changed for the better. People need someone who, in all humility, will bring wisdom, knowledge and discernment to situations and in doing so bring unity, peace and clarity. Every environment is calling out for leadership.

And you know what - you are being called to lead – yes you! Whatever your job title, whatever your status, whatever your contribution has been to those environments to date – you are needed now to lead because every one of those environments needs great leadership. You may be a junior on the bottom rung of the corporate ladder - but you are now called to lead. Not in several years - but now! Maybe you are a parent in a chaotic family – well today you are called to put behind the past and to bring true leadership perhaps even great leadership to one of the greatest environments you could ever lead! So whoever you are, whatever position you hold, and whatever circumstance you are in, the world is calling you to lead. Now is the time to make a difference... now is the time to do something great... now is the time to Start to Lead... and others will manage.

ABOUT THE AUTHOR

Philip Bain, graduated with a First Class honours degree in Business Studies from Ulster University, and became the youngest Marketing Manager at that time at the age of 22. He was awarded the Business Leader of Tomorrow Award by Lord Sainsbury in 2002 and has since gone on to win Entrepreneur of the Year 2010, Young Businessperson 2011 and also won the Nectar Business Award in 2012 presented by Karren Brady from *The Apprentice.*

Having been involved in growing and developing six start-up companies, Philip set up ShredBank in 2007 with his friend and business partner James Carson. It grew rapidly despite the recession and became the largest on-site shredding company in Northern Ireland. Winning twelve awards and becoming an Investors in People Gold Organisation, ShredBank is a local company that has become a world-class organisation. ShredBank also have raised funds for both The Prince's Trust and Alzheimer's Research and are highly committed to their work.

Philip was formerly Chairman of the Chartered Management Institute in Northern Ireland, Chairman of the Institute of Consultants, on the Council of the Northern Ireland Chamber of Commerce and on the Business Advisory Board of Enactus in Ulster University and Queen's University. At any one time Philip is involved in the governance of at least six organisations concurrently and has a wealth of experience in leadership in the private sector, social economy and faith based organisations.

In 2016, Philip is a Chartered Fellow of the Chartered Management Institute, a Council Member of The Prince's Trust in Northern Ireland and a Visiting Professor of Ulster University. He is a regular speaker on the subjects of business growth and entrepreneurship. A committed Christian, he is also an Elder in his local church.

Author of "Start to Grow - An entrepreneur's guide from business idea to early success.", published in 2015.